James II

PROFILES IN POWER

General Editor: Keith Robbins

LLOYD GEORGE
Martin Pugh

HITLER
Ian Kershaw

RICHELIEU
R.J. Knecht

NAPOLEON III
James McMillan

OLIVER CROMWELL
Barry Coward

NASSER
Peter Woodward

GUSTAVUS ADOLPHUS
(2nd Edn)
Michael Roberts

CHURCHILL
Keith Robbins

DE GAULLE
Andrew Shennan

FRANCO
Sheelagh Ellwood

JUÁREZ
Brian Hamnett

ALEXANDER I
Janet M. Hartley

MACMILLAN
John Turner

JOSEPH II
T.C.W. Blanning

ATATÜRK
A.L. Macfie

CAVOUR
Harry Hearder

DISRAELI
Ian Machin

CASTRO (2nd Edn)
Sebastian Balfour

PETER THE GREAT
(2nd Edn)
M.S. Anderson

FRANCIS JOSEPH
Stephen Beller

NAPOLEON
Geoffrey Ellis

KENNEDY
Hugh Brogan

ATTLEE
Robert Pearce

PÉTAIN
Nicholas Atkin

THE ELDER PITT
Marie Peters

CATHERINE DE' MEDICI
R.J. Knecht

GORBACHEV
Martin McCauley

JAMES VI AND I
Roger Lockyer

ELIZABETH I (2nd Edn)
Christopher Haigh

MAO
S.G. Breslin

BURGHLEY
Michael A.R. Graves

NEHRU
Judith M. Brown

ROBESPIERRE
John Hardman

LENIN
Beryl Williams

WILLIAM PENN
Mary K. Geiter

THE YOUNGER PITT
Michael Duffy

KAISER WILHELM II
Christopher Clark

TANAKA
David Babb

PORFIRIO DÍAZ
Paul Garner

CATHERINE THE GREAT
Simon Dixon

James II

W.A. Speck

an imprint of **Pearson Education**

London • New York • Toronto • Sydney • Tokyo • Singapore • Hong Kong

New Delhi • Cape Town • Madrid • Stockholm • Paris • Amsterdam

Munich • Milan

PEARSON EDUCATION LIMITED

Head Office:
Edinburgh Gate
Harlow CM20 2JE
Tel: +44 (0)1279 623623
Fax: +44 (0)1279 431059

London Office:
128 Long Acre
London WC2E 9AN
Tel: +44 (0)20 7447 2000
Fax: +44 (0)20 7240 5771
Website: www.history-minds.com

———————————————

First published in Great Britain in 2002

© Pearson Education Limited 2002

The right of W.A. Speck to be identified as Author
of this Work has been asserted by him in accordance
with the Copyright, Designs and Patents Act 1988.

ISBN 0 582 28712 X

British Library Cataloguing in Publication Data
A CIP catalogue record for this book can be obtained from the British Library

Library of Congress Cataloging in Publication Data
A CIP catalog record for this book can be obtained from the
Library of Congress

10 9 8 7 6 5 4 3 2 1

Typeset by Fakenham Photosetting Limited, Fakenham, Norfolk
Printed and bound in Malaysia

The Publishers' policy is to use paper manufactured from sustainable forests.

For Annie and Ellie

CONTENTS

✛

Preface

I received the invitation to contribute this volume to 'Profiles in Power' from the General Editor, Professor Keith Robbins, and from Mr Andrew MacLennan, at the time Editorial Director of the Academic Department in Longman Higher Education. I wish to thank them both for extending it to me. Andrew has now, alas, retired from Messrs Longman, subsequently to its becoming an imprint of Pearson Education. He once characteristically expressed the wish to see the book 'before I finally hang up my clogs!' I regret that I was unable to complete it in time, and apologise to him and to Keith for having to extend the date for delivery beyond the original deadline. The latter's forbearance, and that of Heather McCallum, Andrew's successor as Editor-in-Chief at Pearson Education, in agreeing to delays was greatly appreciated.

I had thought that taking early retirement from Leeds University in 1997 would free me to devote more than enough time to complete the book on schedule. However, I have found myself distracted by developments I did not envisage when I signed the contract. One was to be elected to the presidency of the Historical Association for three years in 1999. While I am very grateful for this honour, and enjoy the commitments it requires me to undertake, these have involved considerable travel visiting local branches of the Association to give lectures. I would like to think that those I gave on the Glorious Revolution clarified my thinking on the reign of James II, and helped to improve this book. Another unexpected interruption to my schedule was my appointment to a Visiting Professorship at the Carlisle campus of the University of Northumbria in September 2000. Again, while I am delighted to thank my new colleagues for their generous gesture, it involved a move from Yorkshire to Cumbria which unsettled me for longer than I had anticipated. I have now settled down in Carlisle, and benefit greatly from the facilities offered by my new institution, which have been of enormous help to me in the final stages of preparing this book for publication.

Help has also been forthcoming from others. My friend and former colleague at Leeds, David Parker, invited me to contribute an essay on '1688' to a collection of essays which he edited, *Revolutions and the Revolutionary Tradition in the West* (2000). The seminar which he organised at the University of Birmingham, which other contributors to the volume attended, was a stimulating exchange of views, which deepened my knowledge of the significance of the Glorious Revolution. John Morrill and Tim Wales helped to consolidate my ideas about James II, with their incisive comments on a brief life of the king I submitted to the forthcoming new *Dictionary of National Biography*. Andrew Barclay, whose Cambridge PhD thesis on James's household has thrown fresh light on his reign, kindly allowed me to read ahead of publication an article which summarises his main conclusions: 'James II's "Catholic" court'. Mary Geiter discussed James with me on countless occasions. She contributed *William Penn* to this series of 'Profiles in Power', and her unique appreciation of Penn's role in the events of the reign has greatly assisted my own understanding of them. Mary tried to keep me on the right lines. If I have nevertheless gone off them, then I have only myself to blame.

Carlisle, June 2001

Abbreviations

✣

Balcarres	Colin, Earl of Balcarres, *Memoirs touching the Revolution in Scotland* (Edinburgh, 1841)
BL	British Library
Burnet, *History*	Gilbert Burnet, *History of his own Time* (6 vols, Oxford, 1833)
Callow, *Making of James II*	John Callow, *The Making of King James II: The formative years of a fallen king* (Stroud, 2000)
Clarke, *Life*	J.S. Clarke, *The Life of James II* (2 vols, London, 1816)
CSPD	*Calendar of State Papers Domestic*
Davies, *Papers of Devotion*	Godfrey Davies, ed., *Papers of Devotion of James II* (Oxford, 1925)
Fountainhall	*Historical Notices of Scottish Affairs selected from the manuscripts of Sir John Lauder of Fountainhall* (2 vols, Edinburgh, 1848)
Hamilton Archives	Rosalind K. Marshall, *A Calendar of the correspondence in the Hamilton Archives at Lennoxlove* (PhD thesis, Edinburgh, 1970)
HMC	Historical Manuscripts Commission
Memoirs	*The Memoirs of James II: His Campaigns as Duke of York 1652–1660*, ed. A. Lytton Sells (Bloomington, Indiana, 1962)
Memoirs of Ailesbury	Thomas Bruce, earl of Ailesbury, *Memoirs*, ed. W.E. Buckley (2 vols, Edinburgh, 1890)
The Memoirs of Sir John Reresby	Andrew Browning, ed., *The Memoirs of Sir John Reresby* (2nd edition edited by Mary K. Geiter and W.A. Speck, London, 1991)
Morrice MSS	Dr Williams' Library, Morrice MSS (Entering Books of Roger Morrice)

PRO	Public Record Office
Singer	*The Correspondence of Henry Hyde, earl of Clarendon*, ed. W.S. Singer (2 vols, Oxford, 1828)

Note on dates

The Julian or Old Style Calendar used in England in the seventeenth century was ten days behind the Gregorian or New Style Calendar employed in Europe. Old Style dates have been used throughout, though the year has been taken to have started on 1 January and not, as contemporaries officially began it, on 25 March.

Prologue

'A great king with strong armies and mighty fleets, a vast treasure and powerful allies fell all at once', remarked Bishop Burnet of the sudden collapse of James II's power. 'And his whole strength, like a spider's web, was so irrevocably broken with a touch, that he was never able to retrieve what for want of judgement and heart he threw up in a day'.[1] Burnet here placed the blame for the king's downfall squarely upon the king himself, attributing it to his 'want of judgement and heart'. Had James judged the situation more realistically, it is implied, or had he even had the courage to face up to his enemies, he might have retained his crown. The implication is intriguing, since James is often written off as a loser whose rigid religious policies inevitably provoked a backlash which toppled him from the throne. For a hostile contemporary to concede that he might have retained his kingdom invites a reappraisal of his role in the Revolution of 1688.

Burnet was right to blame James for his own predicament. Although the Bill of Rights accused James of endeavouring 'to subvert and extirpate the Protestant religion and the laws and liberties of this kingdom ... by the assistance of divers evil counsellors, judges and ministers employed by him', this was little more than a pious convention. It had become a constitutional commonplace under the Stuarts that kings were not directly accountable for their actions, but that responsibility lay with their ministers. This merely ensured that the only way that kings could be criticised was to attribute any action alleged to be arbitrary or unconstitutional to their advisers. James was quite convinced that this was nothing more than a ruse. Thus of Sir John Hotham's refusal to admit Charles I into Hull in 1642, he observed that he 'fell upon the old common place of declaring against evil counsellors with such canting expressions as were generally in use amongst that party'.[2]

James was of course given advice by several men. In England he was advised by such courtiers as the earls of Rochester and Sunderland, Judge Jeffreys, the Catholic Father Petre and the Quaker William Penn, all of

1

whom were no doubt implied in the Bill's indictment. When dealing with Scottish affairs he relied on the earl of Melfort, and with Irish on the earl of Tyrconnel, both of whom have been criticised for misleading the king about his prospects in Scotland and Ireland. But the truth of the matter was that they were just advisers. James himself was determined to be king indeed and to make the key decisions. It is a mistake many historians have made to try to attribute the king's 'policies', to use an anachronistic term, to anybody else.

What those policies were has long been a subject of debate. A view of James held by his opponents at the time and by whig historians thereafter took it for granted that he aimed at 'Popery and arbitrary power'. By popery they did not mean Catholicism merely as a religious creed, though that was bad enough to most Protestants. Rather it was the allegiance of Catholics to Rome which allegedly made their religion a threat to English liberties. For the Pope was a foreign potentate who was held to be committed to using every device to bring England back to the true faith. James himself was charged with the same ambition the moment he publicly revealed his conversion to the Church of Rome in 1673. Any disclaimer of this was disregarded, as Papists were held to be capable of equivocating to the point of lying if that means would achieve the end of a counter-Reformation. It was widely believed that they received dispensations annulling any penalties for perjury. The king could assert that he genuinely believed in religious toleration, and did not wish to thrust his religion upon his subjects; but many of them would never bring themselves to trust his word, simply because the word of a Papist was not to be trusted. The legend thereby arose that he sought the forcible conversion of his subjects to Catholicism. When he demonstrated a commitment to toleration by granting a Declaration of Indulgence which relieved Protestant nonconformists as well as Catholics from the penal laws, it was taken to be a deliberate ploy to lull them into a false sense of security. James insisted in it that 'we humbly thank Almighty God it is and hath of long time been our constant sense and opinion ... that conscience ought not to be constrained nor people constrained in matters of mere religion'.[3] Yet even this categorical statement was widely greeted with cynicism. In *A Letter to a Dissenter* the marquis of Halifax compared the king to a bear hugging the Protestants the better to squeeze them later. 'The other day you were sons of Belial', he warned the dissenters, 'now you are angels of light'.[4]

James was also accused of aiming, like all Catholic kings, at arbitrary power. Arbitrariness was not necessarily the same as absolutism. It meant ruling with disregard for the law. It was held that there was a rule of law to which even kings were subject. This was not just enshrined in Acts of Parliament but in the common law of the land. The use of their prerogative by the Stuarts to overcome statutes and legal precedents established in the common law courts was seen as an attack on the constitution. For example, the issuing of dispensations to individual Catholics granting them immunity from prosecution for breaches of the Test Act was seen as an arbitrary act since it challenged both statute and common law. It not only undermined the statutory requirement to take communion in the Church of England to qualify for office under the Crown, but also called into question verdicts in court cases which had ruled that the king could not dispense a subject from the obligations of an Act of Parliament if, for example, it injured a third party.

In reaction to these criticisms James has been seen as a ruler enlightened before his time with views of religious toleration. The king genuinely believed in liberty of conscience. It was essential for the religious well-being of his subjects. But it also stimulated trade, as the example of the Dutch had shown; by contrast, Louis XIV's persecution of the Huguenots had been detrimental to the French economy. As James pointed out in the instructions he gave to judges going on circuit in 1688, toleration 'had already much increased the trade at home', and if continued would make the country 'the chief seat of trade in Christendom'.[5] He did not seek to force Catholicism on his subjects, but simply to achieve toleration for them and other non-Anglicans. In so far as he employed the royal prerogative to achieve this goal it was as a means to an end, not an end in itself. If the overwhelmingly Anglican parliament elected in 1685 had been prepared to cooperate with his policies he would have had no need to fall back on the suspending and dispensing powers. Instead, the intransigence of the two Houses had shown that it was the Anglicans who remained bigots, refusing to go along with an enlightened monarch intent on achieving toleration. He had been forced to issue dispensations to Catholics and Protestants granting them immunity from prosecution for breaches of the penal laws and ultimately to promulgate an edict suspending the laws altogether.

Was James a bigoted Catholic or an enlightened ruler? Did he aim at absolutism? This study seeks to answer these questions. Like all the titles in this 'Profiles in Power' series, this is not a biography of James II, much less a 'life and times'. In order to answer the questions, however, some appreciation of the historical context in which James II exercised power is indispensable.

Few outside Northern Ireland today can appreciate the animosity which divided Catholics, or Papists as they were significantly dubbed, from Protestants. The Unionist slogan 'Home rule is Rome rule' goes to the heart of the matter. Roman Catholics were held to place a higher premium on their loyalty to the Pope than they did to their country. They were agents of a foreign power. Hence Elizabethan statute law had made it treason to try to convert subjects of the English crown to Catholicism. Catholics were also held to prefer arbitrary power to limited monarchy, and therefore to be inimical to the 'liberties of Englishmen'. It was the perceived influence of Charles I's Catholic queen, James's mother Henrietta Maria, which led his Protestant subjects to suspect a plot to undermine their constitutional freedoms, and this did much to bring about the atmosphere of paranoia which preceded the civil war between the king and his parliament which broke out in 1642. This atmosphere was poisoned by the uprising in Ireland in 1641. Bloodcurdling stories of atrocities committed by Catholics against Protestants quickly escalated into a lurid legend of a 'massacre'. It fed the fantasies of English Protestants about the cruelty of 'papists' towards them ever since the Reformation. Foxe's *Book of Martyrs* preserved the memory of those who had been burned as heretics in the fires at Smithfield during Bloody Mary's reign. The Gunpowder Plot of 1605, when Guy Fawkes and his accomplices sought to blow up king, Lords and Commons, and would have succeeded had not Providence discovered their hellish conspiracy, was further proof of their inhuman malice. Now they had sought to ethnically cleanse Ireland of its Protestant inhabitants. The Irish rebellion indeed made civil war in England inevitable, since it had to be suppressed. The question then arose: who was to command the army raised to suppress it – the king or parliament? It was over this question that the royalist and parliamentary sides were adopted which were to fight in the civil wars of 1642–1646, and 1648.

The wars also brought out the divisions in Protestant ranks which had previously been largely contained within the Church of England. Charles I had encouraged the advancement of a so-called Arminian element in the Church led by Archbishop Laud. The name was used as a term of abuse implying that those preferred by the king were followers of the Dutch theologian Arminius, whose doctrines had been condemned at the Synod of Dordrecht in 1618. He was alleged by his detractors to have qualified the Calvinist doctrine of the predestination of the elect by introducing an element of freewill and justification by works as well as by faith alone. Although Laud protested that he was not a disciple of Arminius, he was associated with a crypto-Catholic policy of tempering the austerity of Calvinism by introducing the 'beauty of holiness'. Thus in 'Arminian' churches the plain communion table was removed from the transept to the chancel, adorned with candles and the crucifix and revered as an altar. Those who objected to these practices were dismissed as 'Puritans' by those who approved of them.

Puritans were those who wanted a more thorough godly reformation than the Elizabethan church settlement had produced. Although they welcomed the doctrinal aspects of it as being largely along Calvinist lines, they scrupled at some three or four of the Thirty-nine Articles which seemed to them to lack scriptural sanction, for true Puritans insisted that all religious observances should be based on the Bible, which to them was literally the word of God. Such liturgical practices as bowing at the name of Jesus, crossing an infant's head in baptism, and exchanging rings in marriage smacked to them of 'relics of Popery'. Perhaps above all they objected to the priesthood being a separate estate, with ministers being distinguished from their flocks by wearing of surplices, and the church itself having a hierarchy dominated by bishops. Under Elizabeth, and even under James I, those who held such views had been for the most part prepared to remain within the established church. They considered that it was reformed sufficiently for them to 'tarry for the magistrate', as they put it, i.e. to wait until the state moved further towards the doctrinal and liturgical model provided by the centre of Calvinism in Geneva. Under Charles I, however, so far from moving in the direction of Geneva it seemed to be reversing towards Rome. Some Puritans were no longer prepared to wait and went across the Atlantic to set up a godly society in Massachusetts. Those who remained took heart when the king summoned the Long Parliament in 1640, seeing in it an instrument of godly reformation. When relations between it and the king broke down in 1642, precipitating civil war, it took the form largely of a religious conflict between the Arminians and the Puritans.

Under the pressure of the war, however, Puritanism disintegrated into a variety of sects. Those who wished to reform the Church of England along Genevan lines emerged as Presbyterians. Others who no longer desired a national church, but preferred each congregation to be responsible for its own affairs, called themselves Independents. These were the major divisions in Puritan ranks, but there were many others: Baptists, Fifth Monarchists, Quakers, Seekers, etc. After the defeat of the king in the first civil war, parliament reformed the Anglican Church on a Presbyterian basis. Bishoprics were abolished, the Thirty-nine Articles were superseded by the Westminster Confession, and the Book of Common Prayer replaced by a Directory of Public Worship. Thus the Church of England became in theory Presbyterian between 1646 and 1660. In practice, however, after the second civil war the Presbyterians in parliament were discredited in the eyes of the army high command, through their attempts to negotiate a settlement with the king. The army 'grandees', as they were called, engineered a purge of parliament in December 1648, removing from it members who were still prepared to do a deal with 'that man of blood' Charles I. Those who remained set up a court of justice which tried the king for treason, found him guilty and condemned him to death in January 1649. The House of Lords was also abolished and a unicameral republic established.

This coup brought to power Independents who did not enforce the Presbyterian settlement, as a result of which there was no policy of requiring ministers to subscribe to the Westminster Confession. Religious anarchy ensued in which the radical sects – Independents, Baptists, Quakers etc. – flourished. Cromwell tolerated this religious diversity, and even admitted the Jews back into England. Only Catholics and Episcopalians were proscribed, though even these appear to have worshipped according to their own creeds in the privacy of country houses. Thus, though many of the former Arminian hierarchy fled abroad, to join the sons of Charles I, Charles and James, in exile, the liturgy of the Book of Common Prayer survived among their followers who remained at home.

When Charles was restored to his father's throne in 1660, James accompanied his brother back home. Although they themselves were committed to toleration, in fact the Restoration religious settlement was very narrowly based. The bishops, the Thirty-nine Articles and the Book of Common Prayer were all brought back. Moreover, those who objected to them were not allowed to worship in peace. An Act of Uniformity was passed requiring all Anglican clergymen to subscribe to all thirty-nine Articles. Those Presbyterian ministers who still found three of them incompatible with Scripture left their livings rather than accept the Articles. They were subjected to Acts which made it an offence for them to reside within five miles of their former livings or to worship separately from the established church. This restoration of an intolerant Church of England was perhaps the most surprising outcome of the events which brought Charles II to the throne. It is still hard to explain, though the intransigence of the Anglican clergy, the desire for revenge against the Puritans on the part of the gentry elected to the Cavalier Parliament in 1661, and the division in the ranks of the non-Anglicans, who now became known as nonconformists or dissenters, contributed to it.

The reversal of fortunes was, however, seen to be precarious. Although with hindsight the restored Church of England seems immensely strong, in fact its adherents felt themselves to be threatened. The cry 'the church in danger' might not have been articulated as a political slogan until after the Glorious Revolution, but it sums up the mood of the members of the established church between 1662 and 1688. They were acutely aware that they owed their privileged position to the state, which had backed it up with statute law. They were also aware that the state had supported a very different church settlement during the Interregnum and that, given changed circumstances, it might do so again. James himself was convinced that 'the Generality of the Church of England at that time' were not 'very averse to Catholick Religion; Many that went under that name had their Religion to chuse, and went to Church for company's sake.' [6] It was in the hopes of contradicting such claims that the church conducted a census of religious affiliations in 1676, known as the Compton census because it was presided over by Henry Compton, bishop of London. It seemed to establish that the vast majority of Charles II's subjects were Anglicans, and that only a tiny minority were Catholics or nonconformists. Catholics indeed accounted for less than 2 per cent of the population. But they appeared more prominent to contemporaries because they had a high profile in the upper reaches of society. When the second Test Act was passed in 1678 deliberately to bar them from parliament, perhaps as many as one-fifth of the peers were excluded from the House of Lords. Probably nearly 10 per cent of the gentry were also Catholics. Hence the fears of Protestants that popery was prevalent among the ruling class, and that a popish king would encourage crypto-Catholics to declare themselves. The Compton census appeared to demonstrate that the proportion of Protestant nonconformists was also no more than 2 per cent of the population, making the Anglicans well over 90 per cent. Though the aggregate figures supported this conclusion, a careful breakdown of them indicates a different picture. In many parishes, ministers had difficulties in distinguishing their parishioners as either Anglicans or Presbyterians. In some, as many as 10 per cent conformed to the Church of England but also attended nonconforming services.[7] Such doubts led the census, the results of which were widely known, ironically not to bolster the confidence of Anglicans but to feed their paranoia. Suspicions about the extent of popery and Puritanism help to explain the fears of a revival of republicanism during the Exclusion crisis of the years 1679 to 1681, and of a Catholic absolutism during the reign of James II.

The Exclusion crisis came about because of the fear of what would happen should a Catholic, as James was known to be by the 1670s, come to the throne. In 1678, Titus Oates stirred up a hornets' nest when he claimed that there was a Catholic conspiracy to kill Charles II and to crown his brother, James, duke of York, as king. This brought to the surface all the paranoid fantasies entertained about Catholics. Since the Restoration, the fire of London in 1666 had been added to the Smithfield fires of Mary's reign, the Gunpowder Plot and the Irish massacre as evidence of their insatiable hatred of the reformed religion. The Monument erected to commemorate the fire was inscribed with a legend ascribing it to 'the treachery and malice of the Popish Faction ... in order to the carrying on their horrid plot for extirpating the Protestant religion and old English liberty and introducing Popery and slavery'. Now another plot with the same aim had been brought to light. Pamphlets fanned the flames, reminding their readers of the burning of heretics in Mary's reign, the Irish rebellion and the fire of London. One invited people to imagine themselves as spectators at the top of the Monument looking out over London when it had become the capital of a Catholic kingdom. 'Casting your eye towards Smithfield imagine you see your own father or your mother or some of your nearest and dearest relations, tied to a stake in the midst of flames, when with hands and eyes lifted up to heaven they scream and cry out to that God for whose cause they die, which was a frequent spectacle the last time Popery reigned amongst us.'[8] Another warned Protestants that they would see 'your daughters ravished by goatish monks, your smaller children tossed upon pikes, or torn limb from limb, whilst you have your own bowels ripped up ... and holy candles made of your grease (which was done within our memory in Ireland) ...'.[9]

The scare over the Popish Plot that ensued led directly to demands from some quarters that the duke should be excluded from the succession and banished from the realm. Those who took this view backed three attempts in three successive parliaments to bar James from coming to the throne. Initially they were called Exclusionists but ultimately they were dubbed whigs. Those who stood by the hereditary principle and opposed the Exclusion bills came to be called tories. Although not all whigs were dissenters by any means, most dissenters were whigs. In the second Exclusion parliament, held in 1680, there was an attempt not only to exclude James but also to modify the Anglican liturgy in order to accommodate, or 'comprehend', Presbyterians in the Church of England. There was even a bill introduced into the Commons to allow Quakers to affirm rather than swear oaths.

These attempts at Protestant reconciliation came to naught when the king first prorogued and then dissolved the parliament. Nevertheless they identified the whigs closely with dissent, and by association with the Puritans of the Interregnum. Whigs were accused of wishing not only to exclude James but also to restore the republic. Although they tried to avoid the question of who would succeed Charles II if the bills became law, it was widely understood that their preferred candidate was the king's illegitimate son the duke of Monmouth. Some, however, were wary of his candidature, especially since Charles refused to acknowledge that he was married to Monmouth's mother. They sought a Protestant successor in William of Orange, the husband of Princess Mary, James's daughter.

While the Exclusion crisis raged, Charles thought it expedient to banish his brother from England. He spent much of 1679 in Brussels. After returning briefly following a scare over the state of the king's health, James went north to Scotland, where he stayed until 1682.

The situation in the northern kingdom, like that in the southern, reflected the legacy of the civil wars, the Interregnum and the Restoration. Scots were the first to rise up against Charles I in the so-called Bishops' Wars. These began as a protest against the king's attempt in 1637 to impose a liturgy akin to that of the Anglican Book of Common Prayer upon the Church of Scotland, and escalated into a full-scale rebellion against the episcopal hierarchy grafted on to the Kirk by the Stuarts. When the General Assembly of the Kirk declared episcopacy abolished, the king sent an army to his northern kingdom, but this was defeated by the rebels. They allied with the parliamentarians in the English civil war, drawing up a Solemn League and Covenant in 1643 which pledged them to establish a Presbyterian church in both countries. English and Scottish commissioners appointed to implement this scheme after the first civil war, however, failed to agree, and when Charles I was executed in 1649 the Scots claimed that it violated the Covenant. In consequence, war was declared between the Scottish Presbyterians and the English republic. Charles II cynically exploited this by subscribing to the Covenant in order to obtain a Scottish alliance. Unfortunately for him, the English, led by Oliver Cromwell, inflicted devastating defeats on the Scots at the battles of Dunbar and Worcester. Charles was forced to flee from the latter in 1651, and went into exile on the continent. Scotland was so subdued that it was forcibly united with the English republic, the Scottish parliament being abolished, while Scots returned members to the parliament at Westminster when Cromwell became Protector. At the Restoration the Scottish parliament was restored, and along with it the bishops. The restoration of episcopacy north of the border was an even more unexpected outcome of the king's return than that of the Church of England. Only members of the established Episcopal Church were allowed to participate fully in public life. Thus only Episcopalians could be returned to the Scottish parliament. The Covenanters protested at the religious settlement, and some of them, known as Cameronians, went into open rebellion against it. Charles II's lieutenant in Scotland, the duke of Lauderdale, kept control of the northern kingdom, rallying the nobility and gentry to the support of the Episcopal Church settlement and subduing the Covenanters. For nearly sixteen years Lauderdale successfully pursued these ends. Then, in 1679, the Cameronians assassinated the archbishop of St Andrews, and proceeded to take control of Glasgow. Lauderdale's regime collapsed, and Charles sent the duke of Monmouth to subdue the rebellion, which he did in the battle of Bothwell Bridge.

This was the legacy which James took over when Charles sent him to Scotland in November 1679. As we shall see, he made a better job of governing the northern kingdom as duke of York than he was to do as James VII.

Religion therefore suffused politics in the Stuart dominions. Religious toleration was a political issue throughout their reigns. Where there was an established church it meant making concessions to other sects. In England, the Church of England would have to make concessions to Catholics and Protestant nonconformists. In Scotland, the restored Kirk, complete with bishops, would have to make concessions to Catholics and Presbyterians. These establishments were not prepared to concede rights to others without a struggle, for they enjoyed not only freedom of worship but political power. In theory, the Church of England had a monopoly of positions in borough corporations, thanks to the Corporation Act of 1661, and under the Crown following the Test Act of 1673. These statutes made communion in the Church of England a requisite qualification for holding office. The Anglican Church had wide support, but north of the border the Episcopal settlement had very little and needed the backing of the Stuarts to protect it from its Presbyterian rivals.

The later Stuarts found themselves at the centre of religious controversy wherever they ruled. This would have presented problems even if their own religion had been unequivocally Anglican. It had already fomented two civil wars and led to a collapse of the traditional ruling class and the subversion of the social order. That these had been restored in 1660 did not guarantee their continuance. Charles II and his brother James would have had their work cut out to avoid their father's fate whatever political stance they adopted. But where, to many, Charles I had died a martyr for the Church of England there was no way that his sons were ready for that role. Charles II's religion will perhaps never be satisfactorily pinned down, as he covered his own beliefs under a layer of cynicism. He definitely died a Catholic, a priest being smuggled into his bedchamber to administer the last rites to him on his deathbed. Quite when he converted to the Catholic faith is unknown, as he kept it to himself. His brother, a much less subtle man, wore his heart on his sleeve, and when his conversion became widely known in 1673 it raised questions not only about the future of the established church but also about the monarchy.

The nature of the monarchy was at the heart of the constitutional conflicts of the seventeenth century. The civil wars were fought as much over the powers of the Crown as they were over religion. At issue was the question of whether the king was accountable for his actions to his subjects. The Stuarts claimed that they ruled by divine, indefeasible hereditary right, and had to account for their behaviour as monarchs to God alone. Some of their subjects begged to differ. Common lawyers like Sir Edward Coke maintained that they were subject to the law, and that if they did not abide by it they ruled arbitrarily. Parliamentarians insisted that the kings, through their ministers, were answerable to parliament. Charles I acknowledged that the monarchy was limited, and that the Lords and the

Commons had a role to play. But that role in his view was to be consulted and give advice. It did not warrant parliamentary restrictions on the royal prerogative. Hence his rejection of the Grand Remonstrance in 1641, and the Nineteen Propositions in 1642, which sought to make him accountable to the two Houses. To the king they stripped him of all his royal prerogatives except the striking of coin. Civil war broke out over this crucial disagreement. Negotiations during the conflict took the form of conditions being put to Charles which would have the effect of making him accountable to parliament. Thus at the end of the first civil war parliamentary leaders wished to negotiate the Newcastle Propositions, while the high command of the New Model Army issued the Heads of the Proposals. Meanwhile, however, a Leveller movement had emerged in the army, backed by the rank and file who had not been involved in the original quarrel. The Levellers sought to make government answerable to the people, as they made clear in their proposals for settling the kingdom, The Agreement of the People. The relative merits of the Heads of the Proposals and the Agreement were discussed at the Putney debates in 1647 between the army grandees and the Levellers. These were chaired by Oliver Cromwell, whose son-in-law Henry Ireton expressed the views held by those who had originally taken arms against Charles I: 'we fought that one man's will should not be law'. Thus the distinction between the sovereignty of the king in parliament and the sovereignty of the people, which was to inform political discourse for at least two centuries, came to the top of the agenda between the civil wars. It had to be temporarily shelved at the start of the second in 1648. When Charles I lost the war, parliament again put on the table conditions for his restoration in the negotiations at Newport on the Isle of Wight. Meanwhile, however, Cromwell and Ireton had come to the conclusion that Charles could not be trusted. They engineered the purge of those parliamentarians who were prepared to negotiate with him, and got the purged parliament to bring the king to trial for treason.

During the period 1649 to 1653, England was ruled by the Rump Parliament, so called because it consisted of the remnant of those left after the army purge. In those years there was no one commanding figure to play the part of a monarch. The rule of the Rump came to an end, however, when Oliver Cromwell forcibly dissolved it. Those who regarded the Commonwealth which existed between the execution of Charles I and the dissolution of the Rump Parliament as a golden age in English history, and wished to restore it, came to be known as supporters of 'the good old cause'. They also accused Cromwell of betraying it through his ambition to become monarch himself. Although he entertained no such ambitions, events forced him to become more and more monarchical. Thus when the Instrument of Government was adopted as the country's constitution in 1654, Cromwell was named as Lord Protector. It is true that this office was meant to be responsible to a Council and ultimately to parliament, imposing conditions on Cromwell which parliamentarians had tried to impose on Charles I, but the Protector dealt with his first parliament as arbitrarily as the king had with those of the 1620s. When the second parliament was purged of Presbyterian opponents of the Protectorate, the remaining members came out strongly in favour of asking Cromwell to accept the crown. The kingship party was supported by lawyers, who argued that English institutions had been established by the medieval and Tudor monarchs, and could only function effectively and legitimately under a king. A prominent member of the party was Anthony Ashley Cooper, who was to become leader of the first whigs in the Exclusion crisis. Cromwell was swayed by these arguments, but in the end declined the offer of the crown, fearing that his old comrades in arms, the New Model grandees, would reject it. Their rejection would place the new regime in jeopardy and play into the hands of Stuart supporters.

Had Cromwell become king, the prospects of a restoration would have been set back. As it was, the chaos following his death in 1658 led rapidly to a situation in which the return of the king was regarded as the only brake on a descent into anarchy. As a result, Charles II was restored without any negotiations over the conditions on which he would rule. The only terms were those he himself offered in the Declaration of Breda. After the lengthy propositions put to his father during the civil wars this was perhaps the most surprising feature of the Restoration. There were, however, tacit assumptions about the nature of the restored monarchy. One was that Charles would not act arbitrarily, but would consult parliament. The king's suspected Catholicism, and his brother's conversion, revived the association of popery and arbitrary power in the 1670s. The Exclusion crisis came about not only over the scare raised by the Popish Plot, but also because of fears that the restored monarchy was a threat to English liberty. This resulted in what some historians prefer to call the Restoration rather than the Exclusion crisis.[10] James himself certainly saw the whigs as using the prospect of his succeeding his brother as a pretext to attack the monarchy itself. 'He was astonished that men of sence did not see that Religion was only the pretence, and that the real contest was about Power and Dominion, that it was the Monarchie they designed to banish.' In his view, republicanism lay behind the whig attack on the succession, and 'the monarchie must be either more absolute or quite abolished'.[11] He thus agreed with the poet John Dryden's notion of the programme of the first whigs, that it was 'the good old cause revived'.[12] How far the Exclusionist whigs led by the earl of Shaftesbury were committed to 'the good old cause' is debated by historians. To the earl's biographer and the historian of 'the first whigs' they were parliamentary monarchists who sought to make kings accountable to parliament.[13] To revisionist historians, however, they were republicans.[14] Dryden was therefore accurate when he claimed that

> Plots true or false are necessary things
> To raise up Commonwealths and ruin kings.

In the first view the whigs advocated the sovereignty of the king in parliament, whereas in the second they were upholders of the sovereignty of the people. In fact both views were held by different elements among the Exclusionists. Shaftesbury, as we have seen, had earlier been among those who wished to offer Cromwell the crown. This was scarcely the policy of an enthusiast for the good old cause. On the other hand, Algernon Sidney did subscribe to the notion of popular sovereignty. Neither was a supporter of the kind of monarchy favoured by Charles or James in the 1680s, when parliament met briefly in 1680, for a few days in 1681, and a few weeks in 1685; for the rest of the decade until 1689 it was not summoned. Limited monarchy, in which kings are answerable to parliament, was simply out of the question for the last four years of Charles II's reign and the last three of James's. This is in sharp contrast to subsequent parliamentary history, as parliament has met every year since the Glorious Revolution, with significant effects on the nature of the monarchy.

Notes and references

1 Burnet, *History*, iii, 1.

2 Ibid., p. 3.

3 *The Stuart Constitution*, ed. J. P. Kenyon (2nd edition, Cambridge, 1986), p. 389.

4 Halifax, *Complete Works*, ed. J. P. Kenyon (London, 1969), p. 107.

5 *Publick Occurrences Truly Stated*, no. 14, 13 March 1688.

6 Clarke, *Life*, i, 443.

7 *The Compton Census of 1676: A critical edition*, ed. Anne Whiteman (Oxford, 1986).

8 C. Blount, 'An Appeal from the Country to the City' (1679), *The Glorious Revolution*, ed. J. Miller (London, 1983), p. 97.

9 Henry Care, 'The Weekly Pacquet of Advice from Rome, or the History of Popery', 19 Nov. 1680, in J. Miller, *Popery and Politics in England 1660–1688* (Cambridge, 1973), p. 75.

10 Jonathan Scott, *Algernon Sidney and the Restoration Crisis* (Cambridge, 1991).

11 Clarke, *Life*, i, 594, 660.

12 Dryden, *Absalom and Achitophel* (1681).

13 K. H. D. Haley, *The First Earl of Shaftesbury* (Oxford, 1968); J. R. Jones, *The First Whigs* (London, 1961).

14 R. Ashcraft, *Revolutionary Politics and Locke's Two Treatises of Government* (London, 1986); Scott, *Algernon Sidney*.

Chapter One

Duke of York

James was born in 1633, the second son of King Charles I and his French queen Henrietta Maria. As a child he enjoyed the apparent security of his father's personal rule, with no overt challenges to the regime. Then that world came tumbling down with the Bishops' war in Scotland, the rebellion in Ireland and the onset of the civil wars in England. James himself fled from London with his parents in 1642. He was actually in Hull when his father was refused entry into the port by Sir John Hotham. He also witnessed the raising of the royal standard at Nottingham and the battle of Edgehill. James took refuge in the court at Oxford, and was even summoned to the House of Lords there as duke of York in 1644. When the city fell in 1646, James was captured by agents of the Long Parliament and taken to London. There his own servants were dismissed from his service, 'not so much as excepting a dwarf whom his Royal Highness was desirous to have retain'd with him'.[1] The duke himself was placed under the care of the earl of Northumberland. After two years in captivity he managed to escape in female disguise down the Thames from London Bridge to Gravesend and then over to Holland. Did he recall his earlier successful flight down the Thames at the age of 14 when he made his abortive attempt to get to France by the same route in December 1688?

James fled initially to Holland, where he stayed with his sister Mary and her husband William II of Orange from April 1648 until January 1649. He then made his way to France to join his mother, and to hear the news that his father had been executed. His métier as a younger son was that of a military man, having already been made Lord High Admiral of England in 1638 and appointed as a colonel in the army in 1643. While he was an infant these appointments were purely nominal. He had enjoyed a brief command over some parliamentary ships which mutinied in June 1648 and placed themselves at his disposal; however, the youthful admiral had not been able to exert his authority over them, and when his brother Charles joined him at The Hague he took over their command.

In September 1649 the royal brothers removed themselves from their mother's influence at St Germain by going to Jersey in the Channel Islands. Charles went to The Hague in January 1650, leaving James behind as governor of Jersey, a position he held until that summer, his first real command. In Jersey he became acquainted with Sir John Berkeley and Sir Edward Carteret who were later to become involved with him in the colonisation of New Jersey. Carteret acted as deputy governor of Jersey under James, whose first experience of government ended when his brother ordered him to join their mother in Paris.

After learning of Charles's defeat at Worcester, James accepted that the royalist cause in England was lost, at least for the time being. He therefore enlisted, at the age of 18, in the army of Louis XIV, who was then a minor. The army was at the time protecting the young king from the Frondeurs, rebels who were allegedly challenging the influence in royal counsels of Cardinal Mazarin. James regarded this as a mere pretext, seeing parallels between the situation in France and that in England, where his father was executed shortly after his own arrival in Paris. Thus of the Fronde he wrote, 'The Crown was reduced to a most deplorable condition ... Few there were who preserved their loyalty to the King, and even they whose interest should have attached them to the safety of the State were the chief instruments of those troubles which distracted it; grounding themselves on that common and plausible pretence which has occasioned so many rebellions in all ages, – namely, the removing evil counsellors from about the person of the king.'[2] James had clearly concluded that demands for the removal of ministers were covert attacks upon the king himself. He criticised the concessions his father made to his opponents, particularly his sacrifice of the earl of Strafford, deducing that they were acts of weakness which led to his downfall and ultimately to his death. He determined never to show signs of such 'weakness' himself when he became king.

James served under Marshal Turenne from 1652 to 1655. He came to admire the great Huguenot commander, who in turn appreciated the young duke's military capabilities, for James proved an able officer, a stickler for discipline but not lacking in valour. His devotion to the military career found expression in his *Memoirs* which largely consist of a detailed compilation of the actions in which he and Turenne were engaged. They do indeed make rather tedious reading, showing an obsession with detail which raises questions about James's ability to discern the wood from the trees even at this stage of his career. When James joined Turenne, the Frondeurs, led by the Prince of Condé, had taken up their position at Etampes. Turenne decided to take the town and James 'was present at this hot attack' and, in the words of Edward Hyde, 'behaved himself with extraordinary courage and gallantry'.[3] The Frondeurs withdrew from Etampes and fell back towards Paris. Turenne fought his way through them and, though he was diverted by invading Spanish troops and another incursion by the treacherous duke of Lorraine, by the end of 1652 he had installed the royal court in the capital. James became Turenne's right-hand man in these engagements, informing him of the enemy's movements since Turenne had poor eyesight.

The summer campaign of 1653 was marked by the siege of Mouzon. James was in the thick of the fighting at this siege, at one time fearing for his life when a shot from the town came close to blowing up three barrels of powder near him. In another incident he was saved from being fired at from the walls only because the governor, according to James, 'knowing me by my Starr, had forbid his men to fire upon the Company'.[4] After a seventeen-day siege, Turenne's troops took Mouzon. Shortly after, Rocroi fell to the Spanish. That year's campaign was then effectively over, so James returned to Paris, in Edward Hyde's words, 'full of reputation and honour'. This view was vindicated by the duke's promotion to the rank of lieutenant-general before the next campaign.

James's main involvement in the campaign of 1654 was at the siege of Arras. In the preliminary skirmishing James was in the front line, and several comrades were shot around him. When the final assault came, he was in command of cavalry on Turenne's left. He advanced towards the town, crossing over the river. Seeing himself outnumbered, he paused for reinforcements, ignoring the duke of Buckingham's exhortations to advance. While he waited, his men joined with others who were plundering the Prince of Lorraine's tent 'so that at last there were none left with me but Officers and the twelve Cornetts', he recorded, 'which being in full sight of the Enemy, I expected every moment to be charg'd and beaten'.[5] He retreated to the river, where he saw a squadron of horse on the other side, and led them across the bridge back towards the town. When the men he had left behind came towards them in full retreat, however, they panicked and fled too. James found it impossible to stop them. The whole episode records not only the confusion of a siege, but also the difficulties facing the newly-promoted lieutenant-general in maintaining control of the men under him. This could be attributed to his youth – he was still only 20 years old – and relative inexperience. But even his own account also raises some doubts about his abilities as a commander, despite the accolades he received from Turenne and others. Maybe James was not as good a military leader as he was made out to be; and maybe in 1688, and again in 1690, when facing the Prince of Orange, he himself realised this. After losing his own men he went back to the bridge, where he came across four squadrons of horse which he took under his command. Turenne ordered James to join him in the final assault on the besiegers, in which they were defeated and Arras relieved. James was then sent to bring the French court to the town. After that the campaign rather petered out, and in the middle of December James returned to Paris.

Before he set out for his last campaign under Turenne in 1655, James wrote a letter to Charles in May expressing interest in a Catholic plot to kill Cromwell. Although nothing came of it, his apparent acceptance of assassination was at odds with the public policy of his brother. James remained consistent in this, for he was prepared to condone a plot to assassinate William III in the 1690s.

In the summer of 1655 the duke joined the French army as it was advancing against the Spanish defences in Hainault towards the River Scheldt. In mid-August they crossed the river on a bridge of boats, and laid siege to Condé. It capitulated on 19 August, so they went on to besiege St Ghislain. James took up quarters in a house so close to the town that it was not fired at, the defenders not supposing that anybody would stay within reach of their guns; 'so that', he observed, 'I remain'd there in great security during the time the Siege lasted'.[6] It lasted only three days before the town was taken. Turenne was now in enemy country, and during the next month he stripped it of all the forage his forces could harvest, James joining in the foraging. Early in November, Turenne was summoned to the court at Compiègne, leaving the army under the command of the duke, as he 'was then the only Lieut Generall remaining with it ... there being no probability of Action'.[7] Meanwhile a treaty between the English Republic and France was concluded, 'by virtue of which', James wrote, 'I was presently to leave the Country'.[8]

In 1656, therefore, James left France and joined his brother in Bruges. He was very reluctant to do so, and even tried to persuade Charles that he would best serve their cause by staying with the French army. Charles, however, insisted that he left their service. He also insisted that James should dismiss his secretary Sir John Berkeley from his service. Charles apparently held Berkeley responsible for James's vacillation over leaving the service of the French. James for his part, though he obediently went to Bruges in September 1656, obstinately took Berkeley with him. There he came under pressure to dismiss his favourite from courtiers like Sir Henry Bennet, who took the king's side in the quarrel. The duke found an ally in his sister Princess Mary of Orange, who visited Bruges in December. She was accompanied by her maid of honour Anne Hyde, whom James had met previously when they paid a visit to France in February, and who was to become his wife. Backed by Mary, James dug in his heels and left the court with Berkeley. At first they headed towards France, but finding it impossible to go through Flanders undetected, went to The Hague instead. This was the first and only time that James defied his brother. He wrote a letter to him apologising for his behaviour, attributing it to 'violent persons' in the king's service, following it up with a list of charges against them. He does not appear to have seen the irony in blaming evil counsellors for the rupture between them, and declaring himself an obedient subject to the king, when in the case of the Frondeurs he dismissed such arguments as hypocrisy. Nor was this dismissal confined to the opponents of Louis XIV. As we have seen, James also accused Charles I's enemies of the same pretence.[9] He was convinced that giving in to demands that ministers should be responsible to parliament had contributed directly to the breakdown of government and ultimately to the king's death. To employ the same argument against his brother as parliamentarians had used against their father, therefore, was to say the least disingenuous. Charles, with calculated magnanimity, sent a message to the duke offering reconciliation, even to the point of allowing him to retain the services of Berkeley, and sending Bennet out of harm's way as his envoy to Madrid. On one crucial point, however, James was brought to heel. He had objected to entering the service of Spain and thereby opposing his old comrades in arms, above all Turenne. On his return to Bruges early in 1657 he enlisted in the Spanish army.

James joined his new comrades in arms in May. He found them to be extremely formal, and clearly lost patience with their inability to react quickly, unlike their French ally the Prince of Condé and the commander of the opposing forces his old friend Turenne. Much of the summer was spent in fruitless marching and countermarching. Then, late in August, the Spaniards laid siege to Ardes, but withdrew to Dunkirk at the approach of Turenne who proceeded to besiege Mardyck. James also fought his fellow Englishmen at the battle of the Dunes in 1658. This was to be his last action in the field until the battle of the Boyne. His heart was not with his new employers, however, for he continued to admire Turenne and to entertain a sneaking regard for the martial valour of his own countrymen.

His military experiences led him to take a soldier's view of the world. To James, the code of honour was central to the bond between the commander-in-chief and his officer corps. Its breach by John Churchill in the crisis of 1688 was to unnerve him more than any other event in the Revolution. He also felt that it was a betrayal of the chain of command, respect for which was crucial not only for military but also for political discipline. As we shall see, his treatment of the disobedient Fellows of Magdalen College, Oxford, was more that of a superior officer condemning insubordination from subalterns than of a king admonishing recalcitrant clergymen. His *Memoirs* show the remarkable degree to which his mind was very much that of a soldier. In them he recorded how, having despaired of returning to England following the failure of Booth's rising in 1659, he was actually preparing to go to Spain in 1660 to be Lord High Admiral there 'when that Voyage was happily prevented by the wonderfull changes which were almost daily produced in England'.[10] Events moved remarkably quickly to the Restoration of his brother as King Charles II and his own return to England and power.

James had lived through turbulent times, from which he deduced several conclusions which affected his view of the political scene. One was that politics were in a constant state of flux: nothing could be taken for granted in a world subject to bewildering changes. Another was that his father had lost his throne, and then his life, because he had not shown sufficient firmness when faced by opposition.

James was to become Lord High Admiral not of Spain but of his native land. There has been much dispute about his impact on the Royal Navy. Where traditionally he was regarded as an effective administrator, in recent years it has been asserted that he had no active interest in naval affairs, leaving them to underlings like Sir William Coventry and Samuel Pepys. However, such views are now at a discount and James must be given responsibility for the condition of the fleet in the years 1660 to 1673. Ironically, he inherited a navy built up to unprecedented strength by the Cromwellian regime, whose primary task had been to prevent a restoration of the Stuarts. The duke of York's management of this resource has been variously judged, from contemporary criticism that he squandered it to modern approval of his efforts, along with those of a Navy Board established to assist him, to ensure that it was properly manned and equipped. The Navy Board consisted of seven men, comprising three commissioners, a treasurer, a surveyor, a comptroller and a clerk of the acts. The first three commissioners were John Lord Berkeley, Sir William Penn, a former admiral in the Commonwealth, and Sir Peter Pett. Later, James's secretary Sir William Coventry became a commissioner. Sir George Carteret was the first treasurer, while the first clerk of the acts was Samuel Pepys. Burnet claimed that their policy of promotion encouraged gentlemen to be advanced at the expense of the ordinary seamen, and that this was to the detriment of the personnel of the navy. The 'tarpaulins' who had been promoted on merit under Cromwell, and who were ideologically inclined towards dissent and republicanism, were replaced by sycophantic courtiers loyal to the Stuarts. According to the historian of the Restoration navy, when stripped of its ideological prejudice there is some truth in this charge. 'Its veteran officer corps, a legacy of the Commonwealth, was purged less drastically than that of the army, though a substantial proportion of royalist "gentlemen officers" was introduced immediately and grew progressively larger in the 1670s and 1680s as the older generation died out.'[11] He acknowledges that Pepys did introduce reforms aimed at making this officer corps more efficient, but in the end money was too tight to maintain the military and naval establishment of the Interregnum. Not only was the New Model Army demobilised but the number of ships in commission was also reduced. In 1660 the Royal Navy comprised over 130 ships whose combined tonnage outstripped that of France and the Dutch Republic combined. However, shipbuilding failed to keep pace with those rivals during the years when James was Lord High Admiral. By the time he resigned in 1673 the navy had been relegated to third place behind the French and the Dutch.

This relative decline was reflected in its performance in the second and third Dutch wars. James was an ardent advocate of the first, on strategic and ideological grounds. He believed that the United Provinces represented a serious threat to the European balance of power; and he was utterly opposed to its Calvinistic republicanism. He also regarded the Dutch as a threat to English commercial interests, which he himself promoted by becoming governor of the Royal Adventurers into Africa in 1664, and in the same year governor of the Royal Fishery Company. These companies were both indirectly aimed at Dutch competition. James challenged the United Provinces directly during the war with the republic which began in 1664 by getting his brother Charles to grant him territories in North America claimed and settled by the Dutch West India Company.[12] James was very actively involved in the second and third Dutch wars. He even went to sea to command the fleet in the battles of Lowestoft in 1665 and Southwold Bay in 1672.

The battle of Lowestoft began in Solebay on 3 June 1665. James in the *Royal Charles* engaged the Dutch admiral Obdam's ship in a gun battle, during which Charles Berkeley, the earl of Falmouth, along with two other officers, were shot dead close by the duke, who was spattered with their blood. After a four hours' bombardment, the Dutch admiral's ship blew up. This was the signal for the other ships in the Dutch fleet to retreat to the Texel with the duke in hot pursuit. When he went to bed that night, however, Henry Brouckner, a member of his household staff, gave orders to slacken sail to wait for the rest of the English fleet to catch up. This curious episode allowed the Dutch to escape. When James learned of his action, Brouckner was dismissed from his service.

The king forbade his brother to take part in any other actions of the second Dutch war, though he remained responsible for naval affairs, presiding over the fiasco of the Dutch raid on the fleet at Chatham in 1667. James blamed a subordinate for the incident. The real scapegoat, however, was the Chancellor, his father-in-law the earl of Clarendon, whose fall from power it precipitated. Although the duke did not get on well with his father-in-law, he defended him in the House of Lords. He also warned Charles that to encourage attacks on his chief minister was a hostage to fortune. In his view, 'the most fatal blow the king gave himself to his power and prerogative was when he sought aid from the House of Commons to destroy the Earl of Clarendon, by that he put the House again in mind of their impeaching privilege which had been wrested out of their hands by the Restoration'.[13] Charles, however, ignored this advice, and sent his brother to inform Clarendon of his dismissal. He also accepted nominations to the Navy Board without consulting James. During the interval between the second and third Dutch wars the king concluded the Secret Treaty of Dover with France, which James disapproved of, as well as the commitment to war with the United Provinces. Where he had been enthusiastic for the previous conflict, he was now apprehensive that war finance would make Charles too dependent upon parliament.

James nevertheless took part in the hostilities, becoming involved in the naval battle at Southwold Bay shortly after the outbreak of the third war in 1672. There, on 28 May, the Dutch fleet under de Ruyter attacked the English so ferociously that James's flagship was crippled and he had to move to another. This in turn was so damaged that he was obliged to abandon it and board a third. By evening, stalemate had been reached, and both fleets drew off. It was the last time that James took part in a sea battle. Charles again insisted that he did not engage the enemy to the danger of his life, and replaced him in command of the fleet with Prince Rupert. The following year James had to resign the post of Lord High Admiral when the Test Act was passed, debarring Catholics from holding office under the Crown.

The date of his conversion to Catholicism is not known. During his exile in France he had actually quarrelled with his mother when she had tried to convert him to her own faith, and endeavoured to keep his younger brother the duke of Gloucester loyal to the Church of England when she made similar attempts upon him. He was nevertheless impressed by the exemplary lives of the Catholics he came to know on the continent. The first seeds of doubt about the Anglican faith were inadvertently planted by a bishop of the established church while he was abroad. The bishop asked James to read a treatise justifying the Church of England's secession from Rome, which James thought proved the reverse. 'This made him more inquisitive after the grounds and manner of the Reformation, so he read all the Historys he could relating to that subject ... After his return to England Dr. Heylin's *History of the Reformation* and the preface to Hooker's *Ecclesiastical Politie* thoroughly convinced him that neither the Church of England, nor Calvin, nor any of the Reformers had power to do what they did.'[14] Although he conformed to the established church in the years following the Restoration, Pepys noted that James was sympathetic to Catholics. Moreover, his first wife, Anne Hyde, became a convert, much to the embarrassment of her father, the first earl of Clarendon, Charles II's Chancellor and the champion of the restored Anglican Church. James's idol Turenne's announcement of his own conversion to Catholicism in 1668 might have hastened James's move towards Rome, for by 1669 he was persuaded that only the Roman Catholic faith could secure salvation. On the death of his wife in 1671,

James protected her from attempts to persuade her to declare herself an Anglican, and helped to preserve her devotion to the Catholic Church. Even then he was not completely committed to it, for he kept her conversion a secret, and did not publish a paper she wrote condemning the Reformation until 1686. Though he resigned as Lord High Admiral rather than abjure his new faith in 1673, he continued to attend services in the Church of England until 1676. In March that year he not only refused to receive Easter communion in the Church of England, but was also alleged to have said that he 'would never more come under the roof of Whitehall chapel, which makes every one say he is a perfect papist'.[15] It was not until then that the Pope accepted that James was a complete convert, and removed his objections to the duke's second marriage to the Catholic Mary of Modena, which had taken place in 1673. After 1676 his commitment to his new faith was complete. He later claimed that what persuaded him were 'the divisions among Protestants and the necessity of an infallible judge to decide controversies, together with some promises which Christ made to his church in general that the gates of hell should not prevail against it and some others made to St Peter, and there being no person that pretends to infallibility but the Bishop of Rome ...'.[16]

His conversion alarmed Protestants, who became aware of it in 1673, when first he resigned from the Admiralty, and then married a 'papist princess', Mary of Modena. The marriage took place by proxy on 20 September 1673 and the new duchess did not arrive in England until 20 November. Meanwhile there were angry demonstrations against the match. The House of Commons even passed an address to the king that the marriage should not be consummated, though quite how Charles was to prevent that is not exactly clear. On 5 November there were more bonfires than usual in London, on one of which the apprentices burned a large effigy of the whore of Babylon, presumably representing Mary as well as Roman Catholicism. The prospect that not only would an avowed Catholic succeed Charles II, but that he would in turn be succeeded by popish progeny, kept the issue alive even after the duke and duchess of York were solemnly united in matrimony by the bishop of Durham. The Commons continued to challenge the crown's prerogative, objecting to the retention of a standing army. According to Lord Conway, 'fear of the duke makes them every day fetter the Crown'.[17] Despite his resignation from the post of Lord High Admiral, it was still widely believed that his counsels were influencing the king behind the scenes. There was some justification in this belief, for James did not relinquish all his posts following the enactment of the Test Act. Thus he continued to be commander-in-chief of the Artillery Company, to which he had been elected in 1660 and was therefore not technically under the Crown, and to command the Lord High Admiral's regiment by the simple expedient of changing its name to the Duke of York's Foot. 'These cosmetic changes worked very well, enabling James to maintain an active involvement with the Army and to keep his hopes of a field command alive', observes John Callow, 'while deflecting potentially destructive criticism away from his own person.'[18]

It could not be deflected, however, when the so-called Popish Plot occurred in 1678. Titus Oates, the chief contriver of the plot, accused Catholics of aiming at killing the king in order to secure the succession of James. Although Oates did not directly accuse the duke of being involved in it, he did express the hope of seeing him hanged as a traitor. Others, notably Edward Fitzharris, did not scruple to charge him with conspiracy to assassinate his own brother. He was vulnerable to charges of complicity with Catholic conspirators when Edward Colman, his wife's secretary, was accused by Oates of being a principal in the Popish Plot.[19] Colman's papers were seized and several incriminating letters, appealing to foreign Catholic powers for financial help for the cause of their co-religionists in England, came to light. In writing some of them he had been following the duke's instructions. Indeed, one lauded James's zeal for 'the conversion of our kingdom which has a long time been oppressed and miserably harrassed with heresy and schism'.[20] He must have spent several uncomfortable days and sleepless nights when Colman was arrested, tried for treason, found guilty and executed. Colman, like himself a convert to Catholicism, had only to turn king's evidence against him to save his own life. Yet he went to his death protesting his innocence.

The outcome of the hysteria was that some peers and a majority of Members of Parliament sought to exclude James from the throne by Act of Parliament in the years 1679 to 1681. These became known as Exclusionists, and were later called whigs. James warned his brother that the effect of the Exclusion bill would be to make the monarchy elective. 'He again reminded him of the late King his father's mistake in the like condescensions.'[21]

Where the whigs sought to exclude him from the throne because he was a Catholic, others tried to persuade him to renounce his Catholicism. On 21 February 1679, the archbishop of Canterbury and the bishop of

Winchester beseeched him in a private interview at St James's to 'quit the communion and guidance of your stepdame the Church of Rome and then return into the bosom of your true, dear and holy mother, the Church of England'.[22] When James declined, the king considered that his continued presence in England would be too sensitive politically and ordered James out of the country. Initially he went to Brussels, where he stayed from March to September. On hearing that his brother had been taken seriously ill at the end of August he rushed back to England. Meanwhile, however, Charles had recovered and ordered James to go out of the kingdom once more, only this time to Scotland. James went there as high commissioner, the king's representative in the northern kingdom. James resided in Edinburgh from October 1679 to March 1682, apart from a spell back in England between February and October 1680. He thus spent almost three years out of his native land.

This second exile strengthened his religious convictions. 'If occasion were', he wrote to Lord Dartmouth who also begged him to renounce Rome, 'I hope God would give me his grace to suffer death for the true Catholic religion as well as banishment.'[23] James in fact was convinced that he had been singled out by Providence to be the means of bringing his benighted countrymen back to the true faith. In his devotions in 1667 he thanked God 'for my making my escape out of the hands of those Rebellious Vilans, who some months after murtherd the King my father, for his protecting me in all the Battalls, Sieges and fights I have been in at sea as well as on land, and delivering me from other dangers ... and for restoring his M[ajesty] in this his Kingdom; for recovering me from the smallpox ...'.[24] During the Exclusion crisis, when whigs tried to exclude him from succeeding to the throne, he became convinced that their failure to achieve their aims was providential. Thus when Fitzharris was tried for treason and executed early in 1681 James saw in it 'the hand of God'.[25]

As duke of York he is generally depicted as being antipathetic to the Protestant dissenters, whom he identified with those who sought to exclude him from the succession and even to banish him from his kingdom. It is true that most dissenters were Exclusionists, and that James considered those behind the Exclusion crisis to be not only opposed to his accession to the throne but also against the monarchy itself. Like his brother, he considered those nonconformists who sought to disturb the peace of the kingdom, and hankered after restoring the Republic of the

Interregnum, to be beyond the pale politically. But James drew a distinction between those who were politically disruptive and others, like the Quakers, who were prepared to live peaceably with their neighbours. The former he was convinced made religion 'only the pretence, and that the real contest was about power and dominion', whereas peaceable dissenters he saw as fellow sufferers with the Catholics.[26] Thus when trying to persuade his daughter Mary to convert to Catholicism he was 'very severe against the Church of England for its cruelty towards dissenters, saying the dissenters can give as good reason for their separating from [it] as [it] can for [its] departure from Rome'.[27] He approved of Charles II's attempts to tolerate dissenters by issuing Declarations of Indulgence in 1662 and again in 1672, a policy he was to adopt himself when he became king. In February 1675 the dissenters of Bristol thanked him for his 'kindness in concerning himself so vigorously for liberty'.[28] In May 1677 the earl of Danby complained that 'he now made it his business to court the sectarys and phenaticks, hopeing therby to strengthen the popish interest'.[29] When he was sent to Scotland as high commissioner in 1679 it was noted that 'he advised the bishops to proceed moderately, and to take no notice of conventicles in houses; and that would put an end to those in the fields'.[30]

The duke travelled north in October, being greeted warmly by his friends but coldly by his opponents. The latter included the Corporation of York, who received a reprimand from the king for their uncivil reception of his brother. James himself took umbrage at the insult, 'which he never forgott afterwards'.[31] By contrast, he received a rapturous reception when he crossed the border at Berwick-upon-Tweed, where the Scottish privy council and hundreds of noblemen and gentlemen turned out to greet him. They 'placed him in a manner on the Throne'.[32] He was to retain the goodwill of the Scots for his achievements as the king's representative in Scotland. 'I live here as cautiously as I can, and am very careful to give offence to none and to have no partialities', he wrote to his close colleague George Legge. 'None shall have occasion to complain of me, and though some of either party here might have hoped I should have showed my partiality for them ... yet I am convinced it was not fit for me to do it, it being no way good for his Majesty's service.'[33]

James was as good as his word. Thus, though he continued the policy of the duke of Lauderdale, his predecessor, as virtual viceroy of the northern kingdom, by supporting the Episcopalians he ended the repression of those Presbyterians who did not pose a threat to the regime. He was even prepared to be more lenient towards the Cameronians, the terrorist wing of the Presbyterians who were openly at war with the king. They had received a major setback shortly before his arrival in Scotland when the duke of Monmouth, Charles II's illegitimate son, had inflicted a military defeat on them at the battle of Bothwell Bridge. It is true that torture was employed to extract confessions from the Cameronians, for which Macaulay condemned James as a sadist. He followed the whig Bishop Burnet's account of the procedure whereby the accused were subjected to the boot on the orders of the Council. 'The sight is so dreadful that, without an order restraining such a number to stay the board would be forsaken. But the duke ... was so far from withdrawing that he looked on all the while with an unmoved indifference, as if he had been to look on some curious experiment.'[34] Yet other accounts stress his humanity. 'His Highness doth carry himself with so great temper and diligence,' wrote a Catholic admirer, 'is so merciful in all penal matters, so impartial in giving his judgement in court, so humble, so civil and obliging to all sorts of people that he hath gained the affection of all understanding and obligable persons.'[35] He even tried to placate the Cameronians. Thus he offered a pardon to six condemned to death for their treason if they would only say God bless the king, but the offer was refused by all but one.

James's conciliatory approach to Scottish issues met with considerable success, building up a body of support in Scotland which encouraged him to entertain hopes of similar backing when he became king. As the Lord Chancellor put it in his address to the Scottish parliament in 1685, 'we all remember with joy how well he left us, and by what easie and gentle wayes he brought about the establishment of that unitie which we were beginning to despaire of'.[36] Indeed, the duke was in a sense the ruler of the northern kingdom while he was in exile there. Thus he used royal patronage to encourage the development of institutions in Scotland, such as the Royal College of Physicians and the Advocates' Library. This was the practical expression of a political ideology which stressed paternalism and order; absolute monarchy allied to a stable hierarchical society. The alliance worked well for James when, in July 1681, he faced a Scottish parliament as the king's high commissioner, for it proved to be remarkably amenable to his wishes. 'There was not much time given to consider things', Burnet remarked, 'for the duke, finding that he was master of a clear majority, drove on everything fast, and put bills on a very short debate to the vote, which went always as he had a mind to it.'[37] He got the

Scottish parliament to pass an Act declaring it high treason to try to alter the strict hereditary succession to the crown. It also willingly voted supply for the upkeep of the armed forces. The duke was determined to build up a strong military presence in Scotland to maintain law and order against the Cameronians, against whom further legislation was passed penalising field conventicles. The only business that proved controversial at the time was the passing of an Act imposing an oath on office holders, members of parliament, clergymen and schoolteachers, and even electors, to adhere to the Protestant religion. James insisted that those taking the oath should also renounce resistance, undertake to defend all the king's prerogatives, and never to try to change the government in church or state. This resulted in a very cumbersome form of words to be sworn, which some maintained were inconsistent with themselves, though those who pushed it through insisted upon the words being understood in their literal sense. Its implementation was to prove very divisive; but for the moment James got his way. He even insisted on administering the controversial oath to privy councillors on 20 September 1681. When the earl of Argyll refused to take it he was arraigned on a charge of high treason, and after being found guilty and sentenced to death made his escape to Holland. 'It was easy for him to do it since he was not kept a close prisoner', James informed the Prince of Orange; 'his life was in no danger which he and his friends knew very well.'[38] To give him the benefit of some doubt, this levity probably indicates that his principal aim was to impress upon the nobility the importance of the oath rather than to eliminate a leading nobleman. Certainly it seems to have concentrated the duke of Hamilton's mind wonderfully, for after some hesitation he took the oath without reservations.

Shortly after the dissolution of the Edinburgh parliament James returned to England. Before settling there he made one more trip north to bring back his wife and daughter. The voyage, in the *Gloucester*, turned out to be a disaster. The ship foundered on a sandbank and sank, with the loss of over a hundred lives. James himself, who managed to get ashore, blamed it on 'the too great presumption of the pilot and his mistaking both his course and distance'.[39] He would have hanged the man immediately, and was clearly put out when he faced a court martial instead. But others, including close colleagues, also attributed the loss of life to the duke's own lack of leadership in the crisis. He initially refused to leave the sinking ship, and then when persuaded to do so insisted upon retrieving a heavy strong-box, probably containing his memoirs. Giving priority to this rather than to rescuing seamen struck eyewitnesses as being culpable. James continued his journey on another ship, arriving in Edinburgh on 7 May. A week later he returned to England with his family.

When he finally got back home, James was in a confident mood. He felt that he had made a better job of governing Scotland than his brother had of ruling England. He had been firm and was convinced that his firmness had been responsible for the support he had received from the ruling classes and their representatives in the Edinburgh parliament. By contrast, in his view, Charles had vacillated and hence had run into difficulties with the Exclusion parliaments.

Charles at last took a firm line in his final four years following the dissolution of the third and final Exclusion parliament in March 1681. He never called another, even though technically he should have done in 1684 by the terms of the Triennial Act passed in 1662. He also presided over the repression of the whigs, whose leaders were indicted and whose supporters were purged from local government. Writs of *quo warranto* were issued against 56 borough corporations between 1682 and 1685, which were followed up by granting them new charters. These gave the king the right to nominate their councils: a power which was used to purge the corporations of whigs and replace them with tories. Dissenters were prosecuted for breach of the penal laws to the point of persecution. How far this 'tory reaction', as it has been called, was a deliberate royal policy, and how far it was a response to pressure from tories in the localities, is a question that has been variously answered. And, in so far as it was an end pursued by the Crown, it is also a moot point how far it reflected Charles II's own determination and how far his resolve was stiffened by the presence of his brother.

The breaking of the whig leadership by the prosecution of the earl of Shaftesbury and the trials of the Rye House plotters was the king's initiative. But the purges in the localities, and the persecution of dissenters, seem to have been more a reaction to pressure from below. Certainly the stringent execution of the penal laws depended on the zeal of local magistrates rather than of the Crown. It was at odds with the tolerant attitude of both Charles II and James II to those nonconformists who did not 'disturb the peace of the kingdom'. Of course it could be argued that many had shown a disposition to disturb that peace even to the point of risking civil war during the Exclusion crisis, and this could have hardened their attitudes. Indeed, Charles openly expressed his determination to enforce the laws against Catholics and nonconformists equally. But James, who could scarcely be as zealous against Catholics, also seems to have disapproved at least of the harassment of Quakers, whom he did not perceive as threatening disturbance, judging by his releasing many from jail in the first year of his own reign. And when he pursued an official policy of toleration as king, he set up a commission to investigate the motives of those who had brought actions against dissenters during the early 1680s. Any who had profited from the portion of fines allotted to informers were pressurised to reimburse their victims.

The extent of his involvement in government following his return from Scotland is difficult to gauge. Burnet claimed that in the last years of Charles II's reign James 'directed all our counsels with so absolute an authority, that the King seemed to have left the government wholly in his hands'.[40] His biographer agreed with Burnet that 'his indefatigableness in business took a great share of the burden off his [brother's] shoulders which his indolent temper made uneasy to him'.[41] However, he also claimed that James had little to do with the purges of the commissions of the peace, the corporations and the county militias. He did, however, take over the duties of the Lord High Admiral again, though without the title in order to evade the Test Act. He also worked closely with the earl of Rochester, a politician he felt had been most loyal to him during his exile. They were appointed to a commission for ecclesiastical appointments, a body which Charles set up to reinforce the links between the Crown and the church. This might seem a strange interest for the Catholic heir to the throne, but James had no doubt that the alliance was crucial to the survival of the monarchy. He had tried to get a dispensation from Rome to continue communicating in the Anglican Church even after his conversion to Catholicism, and was disappointed when one was not forthcoming. Together with Rochester, a staunch High Churchman, he worked on promoting tory clergymen to bishoprics to ensure a loyal episcopal bench when he eventually succeeded to the throne.

He did not have long to wait for that event to occur. In February 1685 his brother had a stroke while shaving, and, after a brief recovery, another stroke ended his life on 6 February. The sycophantic earl of Perth lamented the passing of Charles II, 'a most wise and glorious monarch, an earthly God', whose life had been 'one continued tract of sweetness, clemency, justice and wise moderation'. He then welcomed the accession of 'a prince tho' of a different character, yet such a one as yields to none who ever govern'd'.[42]

> Who understood how to obey and tho his obedience knew no bounds yet can limit his power and commands; and tho he suffered not only patiently but cheerfully, yet retained the generosity of a prince amidst the calamities of his persecutors and from all he has learnt not to do hard things, who has wisdom to govern, skill to command, valour to defend, mercy and clemency to forgive, affection to his people, and frugality to manage his treasure as he has bounty to reward his faithful servants.

Time was to tell whether Perth's prophecies were as questionable as his reminiscences.

Notes and references

1 Clarke, *Life*, i, 30.

2 *Memoirs,* p. 59.

3 *Memoirs,* p. 68; Maurice Ashley, *James II* (London, 1977), p. 35.

4 *Memoirs,* p. 148.

5 *Memoirs,* p. 183.

6 *Memoirs,* p. 211.

7 *Memoirs,* p. 216.

8 *Memoirs,* p. 217.

9 See above, p. 1.

10 *Memoirs,* p. 291.

11 J. D. Davies, 'International relations, war and the armed forces', *The Reigns of Charles II and James VII and II*, ed. L. Glassey (London, 1997), p. 221. See also Davies's *Gentlemen and Tarpaulins: The officers and men of the Restoration Navy* (Oxford, 1991).

12 See below, p. 118.

13 Clarke, *Life*, i, 593.

14 Clarke, *Life*, i, 630.

15 John Spurr, *England in the 1670s* (Oxford, 2001), p. 80.

16 Bodleian Tanner MSS 29 fo. 130: account of the letter James sent to his daughter Mary in January 1688 in an attempt to persuade her to turn Catholic.

17 John Spurr, *England in the 1670s*, p. 55.

18 Callow, *Making of James II,* p. 107.

19 His name is usually spelled Coleman, but see the definitive article based on Colman family

papers by Andrew Barclay, 'The rise of Edward Colman', *Historical Journal* vol. 42 (1999), 109–32.

20 J. Miller, *James II,* p. 88.

21 Clarke, *Life*, i, 614.

22 *The state letters of Henry earl of Clarendon* (2 vols, 1763), ii, 268–76.

23 HMC *Dartmouth*, i, 36.

24 Davies, *Papers of Devotion,* p. 107.

25 HMC, *Dartmouth*, i, 57.

26 Clarke, *Life*, i, 594.

27 Bodleian Tanner MSS 29, fo. 130.

28 John Spurr, *England in the 1670s*, p. 62.

29 *The Memoirs of Sir John Reresby*, p. 121.

30 Burnet, *History,* ii, 300.

31 *The Memoirs of Sir John Reresby*, p. 191.

32 Clarke, *Life*, i, 644. For the measures adopted in Scotland see H. Ouston, '"From Thames to Tweed Departed": The Court of James, Duke of York in Scotland, 1679–82', *The Stuart Court,* ed. Eveline Cruickshanks (Stroud, 2000), pp. 266–79.

33 Callow, *Making of James II*, p. 285.

34 Burnet, *History*, ii, 378.

35 M. V. Hay, *The Enigma of James II* (London, 1938), p. 24.

36 HMC Report 44, *Buccleuch and Queensberry MSS*, p. 146.

37 Burnet, *History*, ii, 306.

38 Callow, *Making of James II*, p. 296. Callow maintains that James's making light of the issue was insincere, pointing out that he had Argyll executed on the same charges in 1685. But by then the earl had been engaged in rebellion, for which he could indubitably have been tried and executed. There was no need to do this since he had been tried and sentenced in 1681.

39 F. C. Turner, *James II* (London, 1948), p. 214. Callow, *Making of James II*, pp. 235–6, claims that the duke himself took over the navigation of the ship from the pilot and was therefore directly responsible for the wreck, but the evidence is unconvincing.

40 Burnet, *History*, iii, 5. Sir John Reresby also claimed that James 'did now chiefly manage affairs'; *The Memoirs of Sir John Reresby*, p. 329.

41 Clarke, *Life*, i, 746.

42 Bodleian Tanner MSS 31, fo. 14.

Chapter Two

James II 1685–1686

'Never king was proclaimed with more applause than he that reigns under the name of James the Second', the earl of Peterborough wrote to Sir Justinian Isham shortly after the accession. 'He has made a speech to the Councell that did charm everybody concerning his intentions of maintaining the Government as it was established in Church and State. I doubt not but to see a happy reign.'[1] The new king actually delivered his first speech to the Privy Council extempore, and it was written down by the earl of Nottingham, who published it after James had approved the wording. 'I have been reported to be a man fond of arbitrary power, but that is not the only falsehood which has been reported of me', he declared. 'And I shall make it my endeavour to preserve this government both in church and state as it is now by law established.' James later regretted giving his approval to the expression that he would endeavour to preserve the church, and wished he had amended the commitment to an undertaking that he would not try to change it. Yet though the speech as published was 'to the unspeakable satisfaction of the Nation', a close reading might have given his subjects pause for thought. The reasons James ascribed for his support of the established church were that its principles were for monarchy 'and that the Members of it have always shewn themselves good and loyal subjects'. That begged the question of what would happen if Anglicans were in his view to act disloyally. He also declared that 'the laws of England are sufficient to make the king as great a monarch as I could wish, and therefore as I will never depart from the just rights and prerogatives of the Crown so I never will invade any man's property'.[2] Again, what was to happen if the royal prerogatives were to clash with property rights? Both questions were to be answered early in his reign in ways which were quickly to rub the shine off the jubilation at his accession.

Three days after he succeeded his brother, he informed the French ambassador that he intended to call a parliament for May. 'Many people will say that I determine too hastily in calling a parliament', he told Barillon, 'but if I waited longer I should lose the merit of it. I know the English; you must not show them any fear in the beginning.'[3] The general election of March 1685 completely reversed the outcome of the three contests held during the Exclusion crisis of 1679 to 1681. Where they had returned whig majorities to the House of Commons only 57 were successful on this occasion. Indeed, the king himself thought that there were only 40 members out of 513 he himself would not have chosen.

The whigs at the time attributed their poor performance to the strenuous efforts made by the court during the tory reaction to ensure that they would not be elected to the next House of Commons. Certainly there had been much rigging of the parliamentary boroughs by the recall of their charters and the issue of new ones in which the king selected the mayor and council. In most borough elections fought on the basis of the new charters tories were successful. These were subjected to massive pressure by the government to secure favourable returns. Secretary of State Sunderland was actively involved in this electoral management, writing to several constituencies to inform them of the king's choice of candidates. One member raised objections to the irregular methods taken by the court in the elections, and though he was not seconded, many secretly shared his views. Burnet later caustically claimed that the outcome of the polls was entirely owing to the machinations of the government. But the results were due to a genuine swing of public opinion as well as to the machinations of the court, as the outcome of the polls in the counties demonstrated. In the third Exclusion parliament elected in 1681 the whigs held 60 of the 92 county seats in England and Wales. Their share of these seats dropped to a mere 8 in 1685. As the tory earl of Ailesbury observed, 'the gentry were generally for us: a great mark of the eyes of the nation being well opened, and so it appeared by the choice throughout the kingdom'.[4] The elections were held in the honeymoon period of James's reign. His Protestant subjects were relieved that the lurid fantasies they had entertained of what would happen when a Papist succeeded to the throne had not happened. 'Heretics' were not burned at Smithfield. Women were not raped by 'goatish monks' or 'savage bog-trotters'. Anglicans might even have been ashamed that they had subscribed to such legends, and perhaps resolved to give a Catholic king the benefit of the doubt after he had promised to preserve the Church of England.

Before the parliament met, James had himself crowned, apparently believing that until then he was not king *de facto* as well as *de jure*. The coronation service took place in Westminster Abbey on 23 April, St George's Day. The ceremony was performed by the archbishop of Canterbury according to the liturgy followed at Charles II's, though with the omission of communion. James, who had worshipped in public as a Catholic for the first time within two days of his accession, could not communicate in the Anglican Church. It was possibly anxiety over how this would be perceived by his subjects which led James to avoid the usual procession from the Tower to the Abbey. There was an anxious moment when the crown slipped on the king's head, which was regarded as an ill omen.

James made a speech at the opening of parliament on 22 May 1685 in which he repeated the assurances he had given the Privy Council that he would defend the Church of England. Meanwhile, however, he had raised apprehensions of his intentions concerning his fellow Catholics by pardoning recusants who had suffered for their support of Charles I in the civil wars. On 26 May the Commons committee on religion recommended that an address be made to the king to publish a proclamation that he would put in execution the penal laws against all dissenters. James took umbrage at this, and summoned the instigators of the recommendation into his presence to warn them in no uncertain terms that if the House made such an address he would reject it out of hand. When he picked up a rumour that the English parliament would only vote revenues for a limited time, in order to keep him dependent upon it, he harangued the members in a speech more typical of his browbeating manner than that which he had given to the Privy Council on his accession. 'This would be a very improper method to take with me', he warned them, 'the best way to engage me to meet you often is to use me well.'[5] They served him well enough to grant him for life the same revenues as his brother had enjoyed, a generosity that many members later regretted. They even retrospectively sanctioned James's collection of the customs voted to Charles for life which he had continued to collect after the late king's death. And they voted more supplies for the suppression of a rebellion in the west of England led by the duke of Monmouth. These swelled the royal revenues from £1,200,000 voted for life to £2,000,000. Although this sum would shrink to the former amount when the period for which the emergency taxes were voted expired, it did mean that when James decided to dispense with parliament he could afford to do so.[6]

Monmouth raised his standard at Lyme Regis on 11 June 1685. Parliament immediately passed an Act of attainder against him, to which

James readily gave his assent. The extra supply voted by the Commons allowed him to increase his armed forces to 20,000 to deal with the rebels. This was necessary since the militia fled at their approach. James even suspected that the local levies were sympathetic to Monmouth's aims. The duke made his aims clearer when he declared that he was king, that James was deposed and the parliament meeting at Westminster was an illegal body. He even accused the king of poisoning Charles II. There was now a pretender to the throne of England. Yet, despite the fact that many had supported Monmouth's cause against James during the Exclusion crisis, the duke got very little support when he challenged the hereditary monarch. The whigs who had backed him before had been well and truly crushed since, but even those who had survived kept their heads down in 1685. Dissenters and others suspected of disaffection to the regime throughout the country were arrested and held without trial until the rebellion was over. The ascendant tories upheld the divine right of James to rule. They shared the sentiments of the corporation of Kendal and deputy lieutenants and justices of the peace of Westmorland who addressed the king deploring the 'most desperate and damnable attempts of those incorrigible sons of rebellion; who ... durst again presume to fight against God and lift up their sacrilegious and bloody hands against his anointed'.[7] Those of James's subjects who did not subscribe to either party's ideology nevertheless preferred the status quo to the perils of another civil war. James had started his reign with promises of retaining the traditional alliance of the church and the Crown, and until he showed signs of reneging on them they were prepared to give him the benefit of the doubt.

Faced by professional troops and with few men of his own, Monmouth nevertheless showed, as he had done in Scotland in 1679, 'the courage of a great captain'. When he learned that a professional force, including six regiments sent from Holland by the Prince of Orange, had been sent down to the West Country under the command of the earl of Feversham to attack him, he abandoned his plan to march to London and tried instead to seize Bristol. Before he could reach the city, however, his advance was intercepted and repulsed at Keynsham. Monmouth's spirits sank when he learned of the defeat of Argyll's rebellion, though Argyll himself had repudiated their joint endeavour on learning that the royal bastard had declared himself king at Taunton. On 3 July he marched to Bridgwater, where he planned a night attack on the king's troops who were three miles away at Sedgemoor. Had it succeeded, 'it was to be feared that the disaffected were soe numerous that they would have risen in other parts of England, to the very hazard of the Crown'.[8] Unfortunately for Monmouth, Feversham's sentries heard their advance when they were within firing range of the royal camp at one o'clock in the morning of 5 July. This gave the regulars just enough warning to resist the rebels. Even then they stood their ground for three hours. The first to break were the cavalry led by Lord Grey. As they fled, Monmouth shouted after them 'cowardly rascals'. The French ambassador Barillon thought that if the cavalry had done its duty as well as the infantry, Monmouth would have won. Instead, the pretender had to flee the field, leaving 400 of his own men dead and 200 of the government forces. He was captured and brought to London where he was executed on 15 July. Before his execution he pleaded for an interview with James which was granted. James himself admitted that he should not have consented to Monmouth's request unless he was prepared to pardon him, which he had no intention of doing. But the duke had indicated that he had something to communicate to the king which concerned a threat to his rule. James apparently thought this might implicate William of Orange in the rebellion. Instead, Monmouth, whose courage had completely deserted him, merely used the interview to grovel for his life. James was unmoved, and the duke was duly executed.

In August, Lord Chief Justice Jeffreys was sent down to the West Country to try the rebels. In less than a month he held courts in Salisbury, Dorchester, Exeter, Taunton and Wells, dealing with 1,336 cases in the space of just nine days of proceedings. Two hundred and fifty of those found guilty were hanged, some outside the very courthouse where other suspects were being tried. Others were sentenced to hard labour in the West Indies, which was a virtual death sentence. Jeffreys was reported as saying that 'he must execute threescore hundred before the Government could be safe'.[9] Ever since the Revolution of 1688 these have been known as the 'Bloody Assizes'. Bishop Burnet claimed that Jeffreys 'was perpetually drunk or in a rage, liker a fury than the zeal of a judge', while James took pleasure in daily reports of the trials, and called the assizes 'Jeffreys' campaign'.[10] In May 1689 Sir Robert Cotton asserted in parliament that 'those in the West did see such a shambles as made them think they had a Turk rather than a Christian to their king'.[11] It has been claimed that, at the time, they aroused little criticism. Although there are few strictly contemporary comments on the brutality of the proceedings, there are enough to show that James, as well as Judge Jeffreys, was held to have shown no mercy to the rebels brought to trial. Lord Chief Justice Herbert, who rode the western circuit the following year, complained about Jeffreys' conduct 'and the rapine'.[12] William of Orange chose to land in Torbay in 1688 partly because that part of the country was 'animated with great resentment from the cruelties exercised on their friends and relations'.[13] Later, both the king and the judge engaged in mutual recriminations. Jeffreys claimed that he was not bloody enough for his master, while James accused him of drawing 'great obloquy upon the king's clemency, not only in the number but in the manner too of several executions, and shewing mercy to so few'.[14] There seems, however, to have been no such animosity between them in the summer of 1685. On the contrary, after his visitation to the west, Jeffreys was appointed Lord Chancellor by James.

The successful crushing of Monmouth's rebellion left James in a much stronger position than that which he had enjoyed at his accession. It seemed as though his enemies had been routed and he could be king indeed. He was convinced that this was providential. As he put it in his speech at the opening of the second session of parliament that November, 'God Almighty be praised by whose blessing that rebellion was suppressed'.[15]

James's confidence led him to throw to the winds the caution he had so far displayed. Soon after his accession he had explained to the French ambassador that he sought to establish for Catholics complete liberty of conscience and freedom of worship. But he added that it was something which could only be achieved with time, and by directing affairs little by little towards that goal.[16] Now his aim went beyond removing penalties on Catholic services which had been placed upon them since Elizabeth's reign. He wanted also to remove obstacles to their holding positions of authority and even power in local and national government which had been imposed since the Restoration of Charles II. Thus the Corporation Act of 1661 had confined offices in borough corporations to communicating Anglicans. The same principle had been applied to positions under the Crown by the Test Act of 1673. These measures had been aimed at all nonconformists from the established church, Protestant as well as Catholic. The second Test Act of 1678 had specifically excluded Catholics from both Houses of Parliament. James was determined to annul these statutory restrictions on the right of his co-religionists to enjoy full civil rights. He had already got round the proscription of Catholics from hold-ing commissions in the army by issuing dispensations granting them immunity from prosecution for breach of the Test Act. Since that Act required all office holders under the Crown to take communion in the Church of England within three months of their appointments, by September 1685 Catholic officers, who could not communicate in a Protestant church, were already disqualified from holding their com-missions under the statute. James nevertheless was determined to retain their services.

It is sometimes said that James was merely seeking toleration for Catholics, and that he has been misjudged by contemporaries and histori-ans alike who accused him of seeking to convert England to Catholicism. While there can be little doubt that he would have preferred his country-men all to become Catholics, James was not ingenuous enough to believe that it could be accomplished. Indeed he could claim very little progress in this regard even in his own court, where there were only five conver-sions during the reign.[17] At the same time he wanted to give power as well as toleration to his Catholic subjects. This would inevitably weaken the notion of a confessional state and even partially disestablish the Church of England. For, as James informed the French ambassador, he wanted to 'establish' the Catholic Church. Such a goal could only be achieved by exploiting the power of the Crown. Again James has been held to have been reluctant to do this, only employing the royal prerogative as a means to the end of removing disabilities from non-Anglicans. Yet there can also be little doubt that James was intent on increasing the power of the Crown as well as extending the scope of religious toleration. This can be seen in his determination to retain the army which had been recruited to take on Monmouth even after the duke's rebellion had been crushed. During the summer of 1685 an army of over 15,000 men was encamped on Hounslow Heath 'to the astonishment of the people of England', according to Sir John Lowther, 'who had not so much in histories heard of anie such thing in time of peace'.[18] In September these troops were scattered throughout the realm, some in garrison towns but many quartered on innkeepers, who were threatened with the loss of their licences if they refused. This was an internal police force to keep English subjects in awe. Those sta-tioned in Bristol were particularly harsh in their dealings with the citizens who were suspected of disloyalty in Monmouth's rebellion. In York the clashes between the soldiers and the citizens were so frequent that in

April 1688 James ordered a regiment stationed in Scotland to march there 'where there had been some tumult against the Messe Priests to mortifie that Town'.[19]

That James sought to augment the power of the Crown, as well as to extend the scope of toleration, was made explicit by his determination to get parliament to repeal the Habeas Corpus Act of 1679 as well as the Test Act. As he informed Barillon, the one had been as destructive of the royal authority as the other had been of the Catholic religion.[20]

In the event, parliament repealed neither Act. On the contrary, when the Houses reconvened early in November, both expressed anxiety about the retention of the standing army in peacetime and the presence in it of Catholic officers. They raised objections to the latter despite James's warning them not to do so. 'Let no man take exception that there are some officers in the Army not qualified according to the Tests for their employments', he told them in his speech opening the session. 'I will deal plainely with you, that after haveing had the benefit of their services in such a time of need and danger, I will neither expose them to disgrace, nor myself to the want of them, if there should be another rebellion to make them necessary to me.'[21] On 12 November, Sir John Maynard opened the debate, saying that

> his Majesty, upon his first succession to the Crown, had made them a solemn gracious promise to govern according to law, which they had so entirely relied on that they had never entertained any suspicion of it in word or thought. But now his Majesty had told them he would establish a standing army and give those commissions to the officers of it, that were unqualified, and this they took to be an alteration of the Government, which knew no force but the militia, and a violation of the said gracious promise.[22]

The following day the Commons resolved that the commissions were illegal, being contrary to the Test Act. They then gave expression to the resolution in an address to the king. James reacted angrily, particularly to the use of the word 'papist'. 'I did not expect such an Address from the House of Commons', he told them, 'having so lately recommended to your consideration the great advantages a good understanding between us had produced in a very short time, and given you warning of Fears and Jealousies among ourselves.'[23] Notwithstanding his anger, the House of Lords also took into consideration the issue of the Catholic officers and set aside a day to discuss it. Before that debate could be held, James convened both Houses on 20 November to tell them that 'for many weighty reasons' he was proroguing the session until February. He was apparently determined to do this, even though a supply bill for £700,000 was still in progress, because he was concerned that the two Houses would put concerted pressure on him to dismiss the officers in question. He was also alarmed by a report that the Lords would ask for the opinion of the judges concerning his right to use the dispensing power to override the Test Act. James felt that they would be inclined to declare it illegal if they were asked by the Lords rather than by himself.

It was remarkable that a body which seemed so subservient to the Crown in its first session had to be prorogued eleven days after the opening of the second. The prorogation showed that even the most loyal peers and MPs would turn if their loyalty were strained. James lost control of the Lords though he personally attended debates, and expressed his displeasure with those noblemen who made speeches against Catholic officers. Jeffreys, who had been appointed Lord Chancellor after his return from the Bloody Assizes, presided over proceedings in the Upper House. His brusque manner might have terrified the rebels but it failed to subdue the peers. On the contrary, a growing number went into opposition, convinced that the king's use of the dispensing power on behalf of his fellow Catholics was illegal. The Commons took a similar view. No amount of management by James's ministers could overcome the fundamental objection to what they considered the abuse of the royal prerogative. The earl of Middleton, who was Secretary of State for the North, and Richard Graham, Viscount Preston, a privy councillor, the king's chief managers in the Commons, were held to have handled the Lower House incompetently; yet the first session went smoothly enough despite attempts to challenge the Court's handling of the elections. Things went wrong in the second session not because of mismanagement, but because members were convinced that the king was breaking his promise to protect the church. It was not only the independent backbenchers who rebelled but ministers, including the Solicitor General. James was outraged by what he regarded as the disobedient behaviour of his own servants, and remonstrated with one of them, Sir John Reresby, who arrived in London the day after a division had been lost by one vote. Attempts were made to restore discipline by dismissing offenders from their posts. The bishop of London was dismissed from the Deanery of the Chapel Royal for leading the opposition in the Lords, while Charles Fox ceased to be Paymaster General of the army for opposing the court in the Commons. All this was to no avail. James might have remembered this when he ultimately dissolved the parliament after frequent prorogations, and sought to pack a succeeding one.

The sudden decision to prorogue parliament left the government uncertain how to proceed to realise the king's objectives. This made his principal adviser and Treasurer the earl of Rochester vulnerable to a challenge from his rival the earl of Sunderland. Rochester dated his downfall from the prorogation, although it did not result in his dismissal for another year. Immediately before that he had been ascendant in the king's counsels. Thus in September he had obtained the lord lieutenancy of Ireland for his brother the earl of Clarendon. Clarendon had also benefited from the dismissal of the marquis of Halifax from the post of Lord Privy Seal. Halifax's other post, that of president of the Council, had, however, gone to Sunderland, who held it along with the secretaryship of state, a sign that he had begun to insinuate himself into James's favour. He achieved this by siding with a Catholic clique at court headed by the queen and the Jesuit Father Petre. It also included Lord Arundel of Wardour, an 80 year old Catholic peer, Lord Belasyse, the earl of Dover and Richard Talbot, whom James had ennobled as earl of Tyrconnel. Another Catholic influential in James's counsels was the earl of Castlemaine, whom he sent to Rome as his envoy early in 1686, when diplomatic representation was resumed with the papacy for the first time since Mary's reign. His opposite number in England, the papal nuncio the comte d'Adda, also influenced the king's counsels. This group was frustrated by the failure to get parliamentary approval for the king's measures in favour of Catholics, and laid the blame on Rochester and his tory allies. James showed his own disapproval of those tories who had opposed the commissions he had granted to Catholics when he struck the bishop of London off the Privy Council. The bishop, as we have noted, had been prominent among those in the House of Lords who had spoken against the king's use of the dispensing power to keep these officers in service. Rochester opposed his dismissal but to no avail. Shortly afterwards, Sunderland undermined the Treasurer by supporting the queen's protest against the ennoblement of Catherine Sedley, James's mistress, as countess of Dorchester. Although the instigator of the peerage was James Grahme, Keeper of the Privy Purse, Rochester had encouraged Sedley's ambitions.[24] The ploy backfired when James, taken aback at his wife's protest, ordered his mistress away from court. The Treasurer's distrust of the French king and inclination to keep on good terms with the Prince of Orange also played into Sunderland's hands. He was aware that James was more inclined to improve relations with Louis XIV, and encouraged better relations with France. These were achieved in a treaty of neutrality signed in March 1687, in which England and France undertook to preserve the peace in North America even if war broke out between the two countries in Europe.

Another sign of Rochester's declining influence was seen in the summer of 1686 when Tyrconnel returned to Ireland from a visit to England with a commission giving him charge of military matters in Ireland. Tyrconnel proceeded to replace 'English' soldiers with 'Irish natives', many of whom spoke only Gaelic, while Clarendon was instructed to alter the judiciary in favour of Catholics 'of old Irish race'. Clarendon was convinced that Tyrconnel, in collusion with the earl of Sunderland, was undermining his position in England, with the queen as well as with the king, and that his tenure of the lord lieutenancy would soon be terminated. His hunch was correct.

Sunderland's stock with the Catholics at court soared when all but one of the twelve judges of the Courts of King's Bench, Common Pleas and Exchequer found in favour of the king's right to issue dispensations from the Test Act. James had been forced to dismiss two judges who were opposed to upholding his dispensing power, and replace them with two more amenable to the royal will. A test case was then brought before the 'twelve gentlemen of the long robe', as they were called. Sir Edward Hales was accused of holding a commission in the army though he had not qualified himself by taking communion in the established church. It was a collusive action brought by his own coachman, Godden. Hales pleaded that he had letters patent under the Great Seal authorising him to retain his commission notwithstanding the Test Act. The case of Godden versus Hales thus brought up the issue of the dispensing power. The majority of the judges came to the conclusion that it was legal for the king to grant dispensations from statute law. Lord Chief Justice Herbert summed up the opinions of the majority. These were 'that the kings of England were sovereign Princes; that the laws of England are the king's laws; that kings have the sole power of dispensing with the penal laws in cases of necessity; that they are the sole judges of the necessity; that they do not derive their power from the people nor can on any account or pretence be lawfully deprived of it; and that therefore the dispensing power was James's inseparable prerogative'. This was held to be a perverse judgement by many of the king's subjects. One compared it to that given by the judges to a Persian king who desired to marry his sister, and asked if this was contrary to the laws. 'They answered they met with no such Law, but they had a law that the king might do what he pleased.'[25] Even the opinion of the single dissentient in the Hales case, Baron Street, was thought to be collusive, to give the appearance of an independence actually lacking in the judicial bench. In fact, although it was politically provocative, it was not legally insupportable. On the contrary, the precedents tended to support the king. The most recent was the case of Thomas versus Sorrell in 1674. Sorrell, a member of the Vintners' Company, was prosecuted for selling wine without a licence. He pleaded that James I had granted a dispensation to members of the company to sell wine without a licence. Judgement, however, was given against him. It was decided that a dispensation which damaged a third party was invalid. James I's dispensation to the Vintners' Company gave its members an unfair advantage over other wine sellers. Consequently 'penal laws, the breach of which are to men's particular damage, cannot be dispensed with'. However, 'when the suit ... is not to the particular advantage of any third person, the King may dispense'. This left it open for James II to issue a dispensation to Hales to hold a commission in the army, notwithstanding his failure to fulfil the requirements of the Test Act. No third party could sue him for damages arising from the dispensation. The verdict in the case of Godden versus Hales was therefore valid.

On the authority of this decision, James proceeded to grant dispensations to appoint more and more Catholics to places under the Crown. In July 1686, four Catholic lords – Arundel, Belasyse, Dover and Powis – were admitted to the Privy Council, boosting Sunderland's influence and diminishing Rochester's.

This process was accelerated by the appointment of a commission for ecclesiastical causes to discipline the Anglican clergy. James himself set it up following the failure of Henry Compton, bishop of London, to silence John Sharp, the dean of St Paul's who had preached a sermon against the Catholic faith. Sharp had disobeyed a proclamation forbidding preaching against Catholicism, 'saying in a sermon that of all Christian religions the Popish was the last he would choose'.[26] James was particularly sensitive about attacks on his religion from Anglican clergymen. In September

1685 he had instructed Sunderland to pass on a complaint from himself to the archbishop of Canterbury about a sermon by a vicar in Chiswick, which had asserted that Papists were liars and hypocrites. He wanted Sancroft to investigate the matter and if it were found to be true 'he thinks the minister ought to be punished'.[27] On 24 May 1686, George Tullie, the sub-dean of York, preached a sermon before Oxford University on the text 'Thou shalt not make to thyself any graven image'. James took offence and commanded the dean and chapter of York to suspend Tullie from preaching.[28] Compton's failure to act in a similar case was a different matter. As a Catholic, the king felt that, even though he was also supreme governor of the Church of England, it was inappropriate for him to deal with an Anglican bishop. He therefore delegated to the commissioners the authority given to the head of the church by the Act of Supremacy. Those appointed were three bishops – the archbishop of Canterbury, who in the event declined to sit on the commission, allegedly on grounds of health, and the bishops of Durham and Rochester; two judges – Lord Chancellor Jeffreys and Lord Chief Justice Herbert; and two peers – Rochester and Sunderland. The bishop of London's case was seen as an attack not just upon Anglicans, but on all Protestants who spoke out against popery. The Presbyterian Roger Morrice noted that 'he is much encouraged and enabled by the Universall concurrence of all the dissenters as well as by all his old friends – for indeed it was never known of late years that so universall an Interest of Churchmen, Trimmers and Dissenters did follow any cause as now follows his'.[29] Great crowds accompanied him to the hearing in support of his cause. This emboldened Compton to defend himself robustly, telling the court that he represented the whole kingdom, whereas the court was illegal, being in breach of the Act of 1641 which had abolished the High Commission. For 'manifest contempts against his Majesty' the bishop was deprived of all his spiritual functions, which were taken over by the commission. Although Rochester sat on it, he, along with the bishop of Rochester and Lord Chief Justice Herbert, held out for a lesser punishment for the bishop than complete suspension from episcopal jurisdiction. Sunderland, with the bishop of Durham and Lord Chancellor Jeffreys, favoured the harsher treatment which had James's backing.

Sunderland gained ground on Rochester by going along with the king's drive to increase Catholic representation in government at all levels. Thus James personally took a leading part in promoting Catholics to commissions of the peace throughout England. On 12 November he attended a meeting of the Privy Council holding a book wherein the names of all the justices of the peace were listed alphabetically. Those down to the letter E were scrutinised, while Arundel, Dover, Powis and Tyrconnel recommended names of Catholics they considered were suitable to be appointed as justices. On 17 November, names after the letter E were considered, and Catholics and soldiers were again added to the commissions.[30]

Rochester, realising that Sunderland was replacing him as the king's favourite minister, made a desperate bid to retain his ascendancy at court by agreeing to consider conversion to Catholicism. In December 1686 a disputation was held between Anglican divines of his choosing and Catholics chosen by the king. Rochester claimed that his Anglican apologists won the day and refused to convert. James then dismissed him from the treasurership and replaced him with a treasury commission. The first lord was nominally Lord Belasyse, whose fellow commissioners were the Catholic Lord Dover and three Anglicans, Lord Godolphin, Sir John Ernle and Sir Stephen Fox. Sidney Godolphin, who was in effect First Lord, was one of the most influential politicians of the later Stuart era. His financial expertise made him almost indispensable for monarchs from Charles II's reign to Anne's. Although he had voted for the second Exclusion bill along with Sunderland, who was dismissed, Charles retained Godolphin's services. His contribution to the politics of the age has been underestimated, perhaps because he left so few traces in the record. But though he was not always in a salient position his presence was felt. He in effect replaced Rochester at the Treasury. Simultaneously, Clarendon was recalled from Ireland and stripped of the lord lieutenancy, which was given to Tyrconnel. Lord Arundel, the octogenarian Catholic, replaced him as Lord Privy Seal.

The dismissal of the Hyde brothers concluded the first phase of James II's reign. Observers had seen Rochester's power slipping to Sunderland over many months. A critical moment had been the crushing of Monmouth's rebellion, upon which James had felt able to move more swiftly and boldly to his goal. The king then found the Anglicans reluctant to go along with him, as they were to show in the second session of the parliament. Rochester in England and especially Clarendon in Ireland had subsequently been held to have impeded the king's policy of promoting Catholics. Contemporaries were nevertheless stunned by their fall, and particularly that of Rochester 'as being the visible head and cement' of 'the Church of England and all its party and Interest'.[31]

Notes and references

1 Northamptonshire Record Office, Isham Correspondence (hereafter IC) 1379.

2 Clarke, *Life*, ii, 4.

3 J. Dalrymple, *Memoirs of Great Britain and Ireland* (2 vols, 1773), appendix, part one, p.103.

4 *Memoirs of Ailesbury*, ii, 100.

5 Clarke, *Life*, ii, 14.

6 C. D. Chandaman, 'The financial settlement in the parliament of 1685', *British Government and Administration: Essays presented to S. B. Chrimes*, ed. H. Hearder and H. Loyn (1974), pp. 144–54. The king also made serious efforts to reduce expenditure on the royal household, decreasing its staff by over one-third, from over 1,000 to about 600. Andrew Peter Barclay, *The impact of James II on the departments of the royal household* (PhD thesis, Cambridge University, 1994).

7 Cumbria Archives Service, Kendal, Fleming MSS 2943.

8 *The Memoirs of Sir John Reresby*, pp. 384–5.

9 Morrice MSS P, p. 491.

10 Burnet, *History*, iii, 59–66.

11 W. Cobbett, *Parliamentary History of England*, v, 256–7.

12 *The Ellis Correspondence*, ed. G. A. Ellis (1829), i, 104. James himself, who went on a nine days' visit to the west in the summer of 1686 which took in Bridgwater, was so revolted by the sight and stench of the heads and quarters of rebels exhibited there that he ordered them to be taken down.

13 *Correspondentie van Willem III en van Hans Willem Bentinck*, ed. N. Japikse (The Hague, 3 vols, 1927–37), II, i, 612.

14 Clarke, *Life*, ii, 43.

15 Clarke, *Life*, ii, 49.

16 PRO 31/3/161, Barillon to Louis XIV, 26 Feb. 1685.

17 Andrew Barclay, 'James II's "Catholic" Court', *1650–1850: Ideas, Aesthetics and Enquiries in the Early Modern Era* (forthcoming). 'James was most disappointed that more did not do so.'

18 Sir John Lowther, *Memoirs of the Reign of James II*, ed. T. Zouch (London, 1808), pp. 13–14.

19 Fountainhall, ii, 865.

20 PRO 31/3/161, Barillon to Louis XIV, 20 Oct. 1685. Barillon later told Louis that both Charles II and James had often told him that government could not subsist with the Habeas Corpus Amendment Act, passed in 1679. However, it was regarded by the English as the most assured foundation of their privileges and liberties. PRO 31/3/162, Barillon to Louis XIV, 10 Dec. 1685.

21 Clarke, *Life*, ii, 49.

22 Morrice MSS P, p. 494.

23 Anchitell Grey, *Debates of the House of Commons from the year 1667 to the year 1694* (10 vols, 1763), viii, 369.

24 Barclay, 'The impact of James II on the departments of the royal household', p. 26. Grahme remains a shadowy figure despite obviously playing a significant part in the events of James II's reign. Besides being Keeper of the Privy Purse he was master of the buckhounds and keeper of Bagshot Park. As the earl of Dorset observed in *A faithful catalogue of our most eminent ninnies* early in 1688: 'the king does whate'er he's bid by Grimes' (i.e. Grahme). Grahme's papers from Levens Hall, Westmorland, are virtually non-existent for the 1680s, but have survived in some bulk for the years after the Revolution, and are now preserved in the Cumbria Archives Service at Kendal. This suggests that the earlier manuscripts were destroyed when he came under suspicion of Jacobitism in the 1690s, and with them probably a vital source for the reign.

25 *The Autobiography of Sir John Bramston*, ed. Lord Braybrooke (London, 1845), p. 232.

26 Northamptonshire Record Office, IC 2252.

27 Bodleian Tanner MSS 31, fos 196–7.

28 *The Life and Times of Anthony Wood*, ed. Andrew Clark (1894), iii, 186. Tullie claimed in 1689 'to be the first clergyman in England who suffered in those days in defence of our religion against Popish superstition and idolatry'.

29 Morrice MSS P, p. 658.

30 Ibid.

31 Morrice MSS Q, p. 1.

Chapter Three

James II 1687–1688

The removal of Clarendon and Rochester early in 1687 is usually seen as a major turning point in James's reign, not only because he turned from Anglican tory advisers to rely on Catholics and sympathisers like Sunderland, but also because he then began to woo the dissenters. But the change was not as sudden or decisive as that as far as dissent was concerned. It is true that on his accession he assured some bishops that 'he would never give any sort of countenance to Dissenters, knowing that it would be faction and not religion'.[1] Yet the distinction he seems to have been making was between those who sought political ends, and therefore would disturb the peace of his kingdom, and those who were simply religious sects. Thus he had come to accept that the Quakers were pacifists who posed no political threat, and showed an interest in cultivating them as early as March 1685. George Whitehead had an audience with him in that month, and procured the release of several hundred Quakers from gaol. On 20 January 1686 James pardoned 1,200 of that sect and released them from prison, thereafter stopping prosecutions of the Friends for recusancy. In May 1686 he sent their leader William Penn to The Hague to ascertain the attitude of the Prince and Princess of Orange towards the repeal of the Test Act. Although the Quaker leader came back with a disappointing answer, James was impressed by his conduct and continued to take his advice on how to gain the cooperation of dissenters. Previously James had considered the nonconformists to be crypto-republicans. He had encouraged their prosecution for breaches of the penal laws. 'The spring and summer of 1686 were later remembered for a severe enforcement of the conventicle acts.'[2] But working with the pacifist Penn had shown that not all of them were a threat to political stability. It seems that the Quaker leader persuaded him that others would live peaceably if granted toleration. Penn recorded that the king 'has ever declared to me it was his opinion that conscience should be free'.[3] In August the

Presbyterian Roger Morrice noted a relaxing of the repression on dissenters, who were granted dispensations against prosecutions for breaches of the penal laws 'and to give them liberty to keepe Conventicles, and to have this so far as lyes in his Majesties power confirmed by Parliament'.[4] 'At the end of November a regular dispensation office was set up, charging 50 shillings a time for the indemnification of a whole family.'[5]

Dispensations did not cover all dissenters, however, and prosecutions for religious offences continued in the opening weeks of 1687. The solution was a general suspension of the penal laws by a Declaration of Indulgence. On 4 April, James issued a Declaration in which he declared that 'it hath of long time been our constant sense and opinion ... that conscience ought not to be constrained nor people forced in matters of mere religion'.[6] The Declaration proclaimed that all penal laws against nonconformists were suspended. Legislation passed in the late sixteenth century had barred them from the universities and the professions, fined them £20 a month for absenting themselves from the established church, and made it treason to attempt to convert anybody to Catholicism. All prosecutions under these laws were immediately halted, and people in prison for infringing them were released. James was convinced that the established church maintained its hold on his subjects only because its monopolies of worship and of power were upheld by the law. He accused Anglicans of being 'like Micannicks in a trade, who are afraid of nothing so much as Interlopers ... which made indifferent persons immahgin their ernest contest about Religion was in reality more for temporal possessions than the faith which was once delivered to the Saints'.[7] This cynical view stemmed from James's conviction that many men adhered to the Church of England for purely material motives since it was the route to preferment in the state. If employments in corporations and under the Crown were to be made available to men of all persuasions, Anglicanism would lose out. His next step, therefore, was to prepare to repeal the Corporation and Test Acts.

After the fall of Rochester he closeted individual peers and members of parliament to sound out their attitudes to his aim of achieving toleration for Catholics. The results were not encouraging. Among the first was the earl of Danby, who not long before had opposed the king's candidate for the Charterhouse on the grounds that the candidate was a Catholic, and that the dispensation James had given him was illegal. James gently rebuked him for this opposition, and pressed him to vote for the repeal of the Test Act in the next session of parliament. Danby humbly advised the king 'to desist from that attempt for I do not believe that you will have near a majority in either House, and it will be neither for your Honour nor your Interest to meet with a baffle in your attempt'. James, clearly stung by this reply, told Danby testily that he did not ask for his advice but for his answer. The earl then replied, 'my answer is that I look upon these Laws as the security of our religion and therefore I cannot concur'.[8] Danby had been out of office since Charles II's reign and resented not being employed by his successor. The king might have concluded that this could account for his intransigence. But even men who held posts under the Crown refused to cooperate. When James interviewed Admiral Herbert, who was a notorious debauchee, he put it to him 'that he had not been so regular a liver as to make the Test a case of conscience', to which the Admiral replied, 'every man has his failing'.[9] Herbert was dismissed from the office of Master of the Robes. Others also lost their places for refusing to comply with the king's request. 'We doe hear every post of so many persons being out of their employments', observed the earl of Chesterfield in March 1687, 'that it seems like the account one has after a battle of those who miscarried in the engagement.'[10] This was a gross exaggeration. Apart from Herbert, only three members of James's household were dismissed.[11] Nevertheless it was clear that closeting was not going to persuade individuals to support the king. James kept on proroguing the session of parliament hoping to gain enough time to convert peers and MPs to his point of view. The first prorogation was from 15 February to 23 April. On 15 February 'there was a good full appearance, it's thought about a third part of the peers and above 150 of the Commoners'.[12] It was the presence of so many in London which made them available for closeting. On 23 April, James prorogued parliament again until November, to give time for the Declaration of Indulgence to have some effect on attitudes towards toleration.

The result was a propaganda battle for the support of the dissenters. The king's supporters claimed that he alone was genuinely committed to toleration, and that the Anglicans were their worst enemies. They encouraged the dissenters to address the king thanking him for the Declaration. The *London Gazette* began to publish addresses in April, and continued to do so for a year, though only 197 were published. The reception of these addresses was stage-managed to give them maximum effect. James himself in person received some of the first to be presented, and gave a speech 'to this effect. Gentlemen I am glad my Declaration has pleased so many of my subjects ... And I do assure you Gentlemen I will maintain it as long as I live and no Counsell whatsoever shall ever prevail with me to the contrary. His Majesty looked and spoak very chearfully and shewed them extraordinary respect by his frequent moving of his hat to them and by the bowing of his body at the end of every passage.'[13] The king's opponents refuted his sincerity, and claimed that the suspending power, on which the Declaration of Indulgence was based, was illegal. Moreover, toleration based on the will of the monarch was very insecure, since it could be revoked if he changed his mind, as Charles II had twice demonstrated. A proposal by four time-serving Anglican bishops to address the king to thank him for the Declaration was vigorously resisted by their episcopal colleagues and the inferior clergy. The latter pointed out that the Church of England was established by law, and thus enjoyed a legal and constitutional status which distinguished it from other Protestant denominations. Unlike them, Anglicans did not constitute a mere sect. To thank the king for his Declaration, even though he promised to maintain the established church, was to put them on a par with the dissenters. Anglicans also tried to dissuade dissenters from addressing to thank James for the Declaration. The most celebrated contribution to the debate, Lord Halifax's *Letter to a Dissenter*, appeared that summer. In it he warned dissenters to resist allying with Catholics. Their offer of an alliance was pure expediency, for 'wine is no more expressly forbid to Mahometans, than giving heretics liberty to the papists'. They sought to use them for their immediate purpose and then to dispense with them.[14]

Catholics and dissenters had an advantage in this war of words which had been denied to them previously, when state censorship had been for the benefit of the Church of England. The Licensing Act, which had been renewed in 1685 after a temporary lapse, required anything intended for publication to be submitted to official censors before it could be printed. Usually Anglican orthodoxy was given an imprimatur, while anything attacking it was banned. But James now operated the censorship to suppress any attack upon Catholicism or dissent, and to give a free rein to Catholic and nonconformist publications which supported his policy of religious toleration. It is sometimes argued that all he sought with that policy was to create a level playing-field in which different sects could compete. But in the case of the press he did not simply remove impediments to non-Anglican publications, but also imposed them on the Church of England. Initially this was with the intention of persuading a new session of the parliament elected in 1685 to support the repeal of the penal laws and Test Act.

Then suddenly, in July 1687, James dissolved parliament. It seems to have been his decision, for Sunderland was taken aback by it, and clearly thought it was not a good idea. What led the king to decide that there was no hope of cultivating a majority of the present House of Commons to favour repeal of the Test Act and penal laws was partly the disappointing result of his closeting of them earlier in the year. But the timing of the dissolution seems to have been in reaction to his learning that the Prince of Orange was encouraging MPs to resist James's pressure. William had despatched an envoy, Dykvelt, in February with instructions to make contact with the king's opponents, and to reassure them that he was opposed to the repeal of the Acts. Before Dykvelt returned to Holland at the end of May he had a private audience with James, in which the king instructed him to ask William categorically for his support of his endeavours to repeal them. William replied to the effect that he was against religious persecution, but against repealing the laws. James's reply to this letter was scathing. He wrote that he was sorry to find that William 'cannot be for taking off all those laws, and the Tests which are so very severe and hard upon all Dissenters from the Church of England; and since what Mr Dyckvelt said to you from me could not alter your mind as to that, I cannot expect that a letter should prevail with you; so that I shall say no more on that subject now'.[15] Knowing that Dykvelt had been intriguing with his opponents, James decided to defeat them by dissolving parliament.

Though Sunderland absented himself from the meeting of the Privy Council in July, when James was encouraged by his Catholic counsellors to dissolve parliament, at the end of the month he was back at court. He seems to have decided that, since parliament had been dissolved, then everything should be done to try to ensure that a general election would result in a House of Commons more inclined to do the king's bidding. Sunderland's hand can be detected behind the preliminary changes in the lord lieutenancies, and the restoration of whigs to London livery companies from which they had been ousted by Charles II. In August he accompanied the king on an electoral tour of the West and the Midlands. They visited Portsmouth, Salisbury, Bath, Bristol, Gloucester, Worcester, Chester, Shrewsbury, Ludlow, Lichfield, Coventry, Banbury and Oxford. In each town, James urged the electors to choose 'such parliament men as would concur with him in settling this liberty as firmly as the Magna Charta had been'.[16] The result, as far as Sunderland was concerned, was to confirm him in his view that the prospects for a compliant parliament were bleak. Although some dissenters indicated their support, the bulk of the gentry were lukewarm or even hostile. But the tour convinced the king that the auguries for an election to his liking were good. 'In most of those places', he claimed, 'they promised to send such members to the ensuing parliament as would be for taking off the penal laws and Test.'[17]

One place where even James cannot have felt that he received a good reception was Oxford. While he was there on 4 September he summoned the Fellows of Magdalen College to an audience at Christ Church. They had defied his instructions to elect a president of his own nomination. In April he had required them to elect a Catholic, Anthony Farmer, but they had chosen John Hough instead. Technically they could claim that Farmer was not a Fellow of either Magdalen or New College as their statutes required, though they were on shaky ground here because there were precedents for bypassing the statutes. In June, therefore, they were haled before the ecclesiastical commissioners to explain their insubordination. They were treated to a typical browbeating by Lord Chancellor Jeffreys, who took a leading part in the investigation. Thus when one of the Fellows, Dr Fairfax, tried to make himself heard, Jeffreys silenced him, saying he was mad. 'You should have been kept in ye College or brought to me in Chancery as a Lunatiq before you came hither,' he bellowed. 'Officers take him away, he is mad.'[18] The Fellows justified their actions on the grounds that they objected to Farmer not because of his religion but on account of his debauchery. He had given money to somebody to procure a naked woman for him. When the king's letter arrived at the college requiring the Fellows to elect him as their president he had been absent at a debauch at the Lobster, a tavern in nearby Abingdon, where he had caused scandal by trying to give a lady a French kiss in public. On 22 June the commission declared Hough's election void, though the nomination of Farmer was dropped in the light of the evidence that he 'was of a troublesome and unpeaceable humour'. In July, James barred the college from making any new elections or admissions to the Fellowship 'till we shall signifie our further pleasure, any statute or constitution to the contrary notwithstanding. And so, expecting obedience, we bid you farewell.'

In August, James sent a mandate to the Fellows to elect Samuel Parker, bishop of Oxford, but they refused to obey it. When he confronted them at Christ Church he commanded them to elect Parker, angrily chiding them for their contumacy. 'You have not dealt with me like Gentlemen', he was reported as saying; 'you have done very uncivilly by me and undutifully.' At this point they kneeled and tried to present him with a petition, but he refused to receive it. Indeed the gesture seems to have made him lose his temper completely. 'You have been a stubborn turbulent college', he protested. 'You have affronted me in this. Is this your Church of England loyalty? ... Get you gone; know I am your King; I will be obeyed; and I command you to be gone. Go and admit the Bishop of Oxon, Head, Principal – what d'ye call it of the Colledge?' It was perhaps indicative of the king's attitude to the college that he had to be reminded that the office was that of president. 'Let them that refuse it look to it', he warned, 'they shall feel the weight of their sovereign's displeasure.'[19] The tale soon got round Oxford and lost nothing in the telling. Three days after the confrontation one don related how the expression that they should feel the weight of the king's displeasure 'goes currantly that he sayd they should feel the heavy hand of a king and last of all upon his recalling them that if they did not obey they should feel ye vengeance of an angry Prince'.[20] When they still refused, the ecclesiastical commission visited the college and deprived Hough of the presidency. Hough made a defiant speech to them, protesting that they had deprived him of his freehold, which was 'illegal unjust and null ... upon which there was a great humme'.[21] Chief Justice Wright told him 'that he was the cause of this rude behaviour by his popular protest ... that now we had brought the civil power over us; that if need were he would use the military'.[22] Hough was bound over on good behaviour for £1,000, and two Fellows for £500 each.

So far from such confrontations giving James pause they seemed to embolden him to proceed down the path he had chosen in July. He was persuaded that the impression of firm government was needed to bring his subjects into line, and that vacillation on the part of his father and his brother had been responsible for their difficulties. On 24 September he held a crucial Privy Council meeting at Windsor to discuss how best to realise the objectives of the Declaration of Indulgence. 'To use the words of our Saviour,' he told the assembled counsellors, 'he should count them against him that were not therein for him.' Anybody in a position under the Crown who opposed his will would be removed. 'That in pursuit hereof he would regulate the corporations of London (and after that all other corporations throughout the Kingdom.' A list of those to be purged in London was put before the Council.[23]

James had embarked on a campaign to pack parliament. He even devised a crude public opinion poll in which three questions were put to the magnates in the localities to test their approval of his policies. Would you, if elected to parliament, vote for repeal of the Test Act and penal laws? Would you vote for candidates pledged to repeal them? Will you support the Declaration of Indulgence by living friendly with those of several persuasions as subjects of the same prince and as good Christians ought to do? These began to be circulated by Sunderland after the Council meeting of 24 September, though it was to take months to sound out opinion throughout the country.

Meanwhile James made positive overtures to the dissenters to persuade them to support his campaign. On 2 November he pricked the list of sheriffs, who would act as returning officers in county elections were a general election to be held within the next twelve months. He himself inserted the names of Catholics in the lists, but he also added many dissenters who had been prominent whigs. One indeed, Edward Stroad, whom he chose to be sheriff of Somerset, had been implicated in Monmouth's rebellion.

Another indication of the king's determination to support dissenters was his response to their complaints about the way informers had battened on them, especially when the Conventicle Act of 1670 permitted them to retain one-third of the fines imposed on them for breaches of it. George Whitehead had been so plagued by a gang of informers in London led by two brothers, George and John Hilton, during the 'tory' reaction of the early 1680s, that in June 1686 he had persuaded the king to investigate their activities. The Hilton gang had been smashed as a result of the subsequent enquiry. This set a precedent for a national commission of enquiry into the handling of monies by informers to establish whether they had been properly accounted for. The setting up of such a commission had been mooted on several occasions, but it was not until October 1687 that the first commissioners were named. Prominent among them was William Penn, who seems to have reinvigorated the initiative taken by his fellow Quaker Whitehead. Of the 365 commissioners who can be identified, most were whigs and dissenters. They began their work in January 1688.[24]

In November 1687 a similar commission for regulation was established to preside over the purging of corporations, with a view to influencing parliamentary elections. Its work was supervised by Sunderland and his ally Jeffreys, together with Catholic regulators including Father Petre, who was also admitted to the Privy Council in November. The most active of the regulators appears to have been Sir Nicholas Butler, another Catholic counsellor.[25] Their instructions were implemented by paid agents, the chief of whom was Robert Brent. The regulators presided over the purging of a thousand officials from borough corporations. In many cases this involved replacing men who had been installed during the 'tory reaction' of the early 1680s with their local rivals, some of them whig exclusionist. Some boroughs were purged again and again. In London the regulation extended to the livery companies, which formed the parliamentary electorate. These too had been purged during the 'tory reaction'. Under their new charters, the Crown had the right to nominate the liverymen. In the purges of Charles II's reign, whigs and dissenters had been removed to be replaced by staunch tories and Anglicans. The result had been the unopposed return of four members from London in the general election of 1685. Now the process was reversed, and the High Church tories were ousted to make room for those who had been removed earlier. The exercise was chaotic enough, but the chaos was compounded by the fact that many of the new charters required the liverymen to take the oaths and tests designed to keep non-Anglicans out of the companies. Although James issued guidelines on 19 November 1687 to the effect that the liverymen need not swear allegiance to the established church, there was still confusion. As Mark Knights observes, 'such cases are testimony to the muddle at the heart of government, symptomatic of a king acting piecemeal and unsystematically'.[26] Those who conducted the purges were nevertheless very sanguine about their producing a parliamentary majority favourable to the repeal of the penal laws and Test Act. By April 1688 they were confident that 'the greatest part by far of those that will be chosen ... will out of inclination readily concur with Your Majesty to abolish those Laws and Tests'.[27] Yet other contemporaries were doubtful. 'By some of the changes which are already made', the earl of Clarendon observed in December 1687, 'it is probable those who are put into those [corporations] will be as averse to what the king would have as those who are put out.'[28]

Whether or not it would have worked is a question which can never be answered satisfactorily, since James abandoned it before it could be tested at the polls. It remains, therefore, hypothetical. Contemporaries were divided about its prospects. The Presbyterian Roger Morrice thought that if 'the sober churchmen' could be persuaded to accept the scheme it could 'put the Government upon a national bottom'. James would then be king 'not of a faction, as his grandfather, father and brother were, but of the whole nation ... and he would be terrible abrode for he would want neither men, money nor fleets to pursue this national bottom'.[29] However, the bulk of the Anglicans were clearly alarmed by the campaign. If it had succeeded it would have made the king's position impregnable, and given statutory weight to his policies. This probably made more people determined to put an end to his regime than any other consideration which led to his downfall.

The prospects for James's attempt to pack parliament have also provoked disagreements among historians.[30] However, every sign of public opinion indicates that his efforts would have been thwarted. The responses to the three questions were not conducive to optimism about the outcome of an election. Only about one-quarter of them indicated that the respondents would vote either for repeal if elected or for candidates pledged to do so. Between one-quarter and one-third were explicitly opposed to repeal. The remainder, who evaded a direct answer by saying they would wait to see what arguments were used when parliament met if elected, or would vote for candidates who would serve the king faithfully and honestly, were implicitly opposed to repeal. Of course it could be argued that public opinion would not have been influential in the majority of small boroughs which returned members to parliament. Here the regulators were prepared to reduce the electorate to a rump which would vote for the king's measures. But even this is to be doubted. Public opinion could not be completely eliminated even from the smallest constituencies when such issues were at stake. This was obvious even to the regulators themselves. In April 1688 they observed 'that Monsr Fagell's Letter and other pamphlets are industriously spread through all parts with discourses and endeavours to prejudice the minds of those who are faithful or inclined to your Majesty's interest'.[31] The regulators clearly thought this propaganda represented a threat to their efforts, for they recommended 'a sufficient number of such other books as may reform and furnish the country with arguments to discover and detect the fallacious subtleties of those pernicious pamphlets'.[32] In the late summer of 1688 they issued a booklet of *Memorandums for those that go into the country to dispose the corporations to a good election of members of parliament to be read by them often.*[33] These were not concerned merely with the mechanics of the regulation, but addressed issues raised by the king's measures. Thus one required them 'to take care to inform those you converse with that liberty of conscience hath been the cause of the Hollanders' great trade, riches and power etc.'. The whole booklet was a public relations exercise to offset the influence of the gentry and the clergy in the constituencies. Whether it would have worked is doubtful. As Sir John Bramston put it: 'people would not be so mad as to send to Parliament such representatives as would cut theire owne throats'.[34]

James himself was becoming increasingly oblivious to public opinion in the last year of his reign. When the queen became pregnant in October 1687 he was convinced that God was on his side and that they would have a son. This conviction led him to become reckless in pursuit of his goals. He was spurred on by the more extreme Catholics at court. There are clear signs that power was slipping from Sunderland to the Catholic ministers. In November the bishop of Ely was dismissed from the post of Lord Almoner which was given to Cardinal Howard. In his absence his duties were to be performed by John Leyburn, vicar apostolic and bishop of Adramitium *in partibus infidelium*, who had been in England since December 1685 exercising canon law jurisdiction over Catholics. In 1688 the king persuaded the Pope to appoint three other vicars apostolic as bishops. He also tried, but failed, to get the Pope to nominate Catholic priests, including Father Petre, as diocesan bishops in England. When the bishop of Oxford died in March 1688, James nominated Bonaventure Gifford, bishop elect of Madaura *in partibus* and vicar apostolic in the Midlands, as the President of Magdalen College Oxford. Obadiah Walker, master of University College, Oxford, had declared himself a Catholic in 1686 and had been granted a dispensation to keep the mastership notwithstanding his conversion from Anglicanism. A Catholic master was installed in Sidney Sussex college, Cambridge, despite the protests of the dons. This intrusion of Catholic presidents on to Oxford and Cambridge colleges was part of a design to put the Catholic Church on an even footing with the Anglican. A visitor to Oxford in the summer of 1688 observed that Gifford 'confirmed a great many last week in the college chapel where they hear Mass daily ... that college is pretty full and all Papists except 2 or 3'.[35] The colleges were designated as seminaries for the training of a Catholic priesthood. It was even rumoured that the see of York, vacant since the death of Archbishop Dolben in 1686, was being prepared for a

Catholic incumbent. That such high-profile schemes to create a Catholic establishment alienated the majority of his subjects did not seem to concern a monarch who felt sure that God was on his side.

That Providence blessed his cause seemed to be confirmed by the birth of a son the following June. 'It has pleased the Almighty', the king informed the States General, 'who is the sole ruler of Princes and who is uniquely capable of perpetuating their families, to bestow his divine bounty on us and our kingdoms by sending us a son.'[36] 'The mercy of God has indulged us with a son', he told the Pope. 'This so much wished for pledge of a succession to our kingdoms has been granted to us by the Benevolent Being.'[37] On 10 June, the day of his son's birth, he issued a Proclamation for public thanksgiving throughout the realm for God's 'great and continued mercy to his Majesty and his Kingdoms' by blessing himself and his queen with a son 'and these his Kingdoms and Dominions with a Prince'. London was to celebrate the birth on 17 June and the rest of the kingdom on 1 July. On 29 June, however, James's confidence in divine Providence was severely shaken when the jury in the Court of King's Bench acquitted seven bishops on a charge of seditious libel.

The trial had arisen as a result of his reissue of the Declaration of Indulgence in April, appending to it the information that parliament was to be summoned in November to enact it. On 4 May, an Order in Council required the clergy to read the Declaration in their churches, while the bishops were instructed to distribute it through their dioceses. It was to be read in London and a radius of ten miles around on 20 and 27 May, and in the rest of the country on 3 and 9 June. This was easily the most crucial decision taken in James's reign. Yet it is hard to attribute responsibility for it. After the fall of Rochester, Sunderland had the most influence on the king. Since then, however, James had recruited Catholic advisers until the balance of power had shifted in his Privy Council. A turning point was the admission of Father Petre 'in his Jesuit habit, to wit a long cloak a cassock and a little band', in November 1687. Sunderland almost certainly did not advise James to have the clergy read the Declaration, while Petre was alleged to have said that the Anglican clergy 'should be made to eat their own dung'.[38] At the same time, dissenters like William Penn and the Independent Stephen Lob were also consulted by the king. Indeed, Lob was alleged to have advised the reading of the Declaration by the clergy, and when they refused James was rumoured to have asked him what he should do next.[39] To look around for who advised the decision, however, as contemporaries did and historians have done, is to overlook the fact that James himself was driving on a policy inspired by the notion that whosoever was not for him was against him. By requiring them to read the Declaration, the king was forcing the Anglicans to put up or shut up.

The result was consternation among the clergy. Led by Bishop Turner of Ely, a group of them determined not to read out the Declaration. Backed by leading London clergy, Turner persuaded six other bishops, including the archbishop of Canterbury, to join him in a petition to the king requesting that he did not insist upon their reading and distributing the Declaration. James, who had promoted most of them, was completely taken aback when he was presented with this petition on 18 May. At first he greeted them smiling, thinking that they merely petitioned against liberty of conscience. But when he read it and saw that it attacked the suspending power, 'his countenance sunk and he looked pale'.[40] 'This is a great surprise to me,' he declared. 'Here are strange words. I did not expect this from you, especially from some of you. This is a standard of rebellion.' When some of them protested that they would die rather than resist him he replied, 'I tell you this is a standard of rebellion. I never saw such an address.' After insisting that they were loyal subjects they begged the king not to insist on the reading of the Declaration. That was a contradiction of his avowed intent of granting liberty of conscience, since Anglicans could not conscientiously obey it. James, obviously unnerved by the whole episode, simply responded, 'I will keep this paper. Tis the strangest address which I ever saw.' The audience concluded with an argument about the legality of the suspending power.[41]

The lead taken by the seven was followed by the inferior clergy. Those in London were the first to show their defiance, since they had been required to read it to their congregations before the rest of the country. When there was near unanimous refusal to do so, clergymen throughout the land were urged to follow the example of their colleagues in the capital. The campaign met with considerable success. In Durham, where the bishop Lord Crewe was a sycophantic time-server, 'not one major or minor canon resident in the Cathedral could be prevail'd with to read his Majestie's Declaration'.[42] The bishop of Carlisle was happy to report that he did 'not believe 'twas read by any one man of this Diocese'.[43] It was calculated that 'of 9000 churches in England but 400 ministers read it'.[44] James blamed the bishops for this widespread defiance and determined to punish them. It was apparently his own decision to have them tried for seditious libel. Sunderland was for milder measures, while Father Petre encouraged the king to make an example of the bishops. As Lord Chancellor Jeffreys put it, 'some men would hurry the king to his destruction'.[45] James even sent the bishops to the Tower for refusing to give recognisances for their appearance in court. When they appeared, they pleaded not guilty to the charge that they had published a false, malicious and seditious libel. It was not false because the matter of the petition was true, since the use of the suspending power, on which the Declaration of Indulgence was based, 'hath often been declared illegal in Parliament'. They thereby brought the issue of the prerogative before the court, which James had been anxious to avoid even though he had a good case. As the bishops pointed out, there were resolutions of the House of Commons against the suspending power. That of 1673 protesting against Charles II's Declaration of Indulgence resolved 'that penal statutes in matters ecclesiastical cannot be suspended but by Act of Parliament'. But declarations of the House of Commons did not make law. The Elizabethan Act of Supremacy, on the other hand, gave the Crown all the authority previously possessed by the Pope, 'and that the Pope had a power to dispense with the penal laws in matters of religion', asserted one pamphleteer, 'was never questioned'.[46]

James wanted the trial to be confined to the charge of seditious libel for publishing the petition. In this he was on safer ground, since the law was clear that any publication concerning the government which did not have its permission to publish was a libel, whether true or false. All the Crown had to do, therefore, was to prove that the bishops had actually published their petition. There were, however, some technical difficulties in proving this, and in the trial the key issue became the way in which the petition had been presented. The bishops insisted that it was not malicious or seditious since they had delivered their petition in a peaceful and legal manner. Counsel for the Crown argued that the petition was seditious since the proper procedure for presenting it was through parliament. When they asserted that the bishops should have waited for the parliament promised in the Declaration to meet in November, they were hissed. None of the four judges who heard the case was prepared to support the king's suspending power. As one of them put it: 'if this be once allowed of, there will need no Parliament; all the legislative will be in the King, which is a thing worth considering'.[47] Indeed, the judges were divided, two directing the jury to find for the Crown, while the other two indicated that they should acquit the bishops. In the event, on 29 June the bishops were acquitted, amidst wide rejoicing. Even the troops encamped at Hounslow Heath cheered, even 'tho' the King was then actually at dinner in the camp; which surprised him extreamly'.[48] Although he had tried to restrict the trial to the issue of libel, the trial was widely seen as vindicating the rule of law against his prerogative. As the dissenter Roger Morrice saw it, the case was that of the 'prince's private will and pleasure against his legal and incontrovertible will'.[49]

A sign of how far the verdict unnerved James was his issuing a Proclamation against 'vice, prophaneness and debauchery', on the very day the verdict was announced. In the Proclamation he vowed 'to exercise the greatest severity of punishment against men of dissolute, debauched and prophane lives of what quality ... soever'. The germ of the thought which was to plague him for the rest of his life seems to have inspired this move – that he was the greatest offender in this respect. His casual infidelities had moved his pregnant queen to shed tears in public. Open immorality, as the Proclamation acknowledged, would forfeit the favourable dispensations of Providence and incur afflicting ones.

James nevertheless continued resolutely, even obstinately, with his campaign. On 1 July he attended the Privy Council, where he angrily announced that he was determined to discover which bishops had not circulated the Declaration and which of the clergy had not read it. The commission for ecclesiastical causes was charged with the task of ascertaining their names. He emphasised his determination to grant equal liberty to all persuasions, repeating the expression three times. When the judges went on circuit that summer, in their charges to the grand juries they publicly denounced the petition of the seven bishops as a libel, even though they had been acquitted. This seems to have been concerted at court before they left London, for those who 'behaved themselves lukewarmly in the matter' were expected to be dismissed.[50]

The king also pressed on with his preparations for a new parliament. He was prepared to make enough peers to give him a majority in the House of Lords. An estimate of the probable voting intentions of the peerage indicated that a majority of between 50 and 60 would defeat any move to repeal the penal laws and Test Act. Were the Catholic peers, who numbered about 25, able to take their seats, the margin of votes would be reduced to at most 35. However, Catholics were effectively barred from parliament by the second Test Act of 1678. James had not issued dispensations from that after obtaining legal advice that it would be unconstitutional to use the dispensing power to circumvent a statute which prescribed the composition of parliament. He therefore needed to create at least 60 new peers to ensure a majority of the Lords would favour of his measures. By 24 August 1688 he was ready to do so. On that day an extraordinary meeting of the Privy Council was held to announce that parliament would be summoned to convene on 27 November and that writs for a general election would be issued on 18 September. It was very much the king's decision. Two prominent members of the factions in the Council, Jeffreys and Petre, both tried to dissuade him from calling a parliament so soon. Notwithstanding, James, 'when they had ended, rose up, and said "But I will have a Parliament"'.[51]

By then he was satisfied that the regulation of elections for the House of Commons had gone far enough to secure a majority in the Lower House too. The regulators assured him that 'we have no reason to doubt but there will be an election of members for the parliament that will readily concur with Your Majesty in establishing the Libertie proposed by Your Majesty's most gracious Declaration'.[52] On 18 September the king issued writs for a general election to take place. Ten days later these writs were hastily recalled as James called off the election in a panic on learning of the Prince of Orange's intentions to invade England.

Notes and references

1 G. V. Bennett, 'The seven bishops: a reconsideration', *Studies in Church History* (1978), vol. xv, 273.

2 Ibid., p. 276.

3 M. V. Hay, *The Enigma of James II* (London, 1938), p. 76.

4 Morrice MSS P, p. 615.

5 Bennett, 'Seven bishops', p. 278.

6 Mary K. Geiter, *William Penn* (London, 2000), pp. 54–6.

7 Clarke, *Life*, ii, 114.

8 Morrice MSS Q, p. 54.

9 PRO 30/53/8, fo. 42. Some contemporaries claimed that many who refused to go along with the king's requests were cashiered. In fact only four royal servants were removed, including Herbert who was dismissed from the post of Master of the Robes.

10 BL Althorp Papers H1, Chesterfield to Halifax, 15 March 1687.

11 Lords Maynard and Newport and Henry Savile lost the posts of comptroller and treasurer of

the household and vice chamberlain. Andrew Peter Barclay, 'The impact of James II on the departments of the royal household', PhD thesis, Cambridge, 1994, p. 131.

12 Morrice MSS Q, p. 71.

13 Ibid., p. 115.

14 Halifax, *Complete Works*, ed. J. P. Kenyon (London, 1969), pp. 106, 111, 113.

15 Sir John Dalrymple, *Memoirs of Great Britain and Ireland* (2 vols, 1773), ii, appendix part the first, p. 185.

16 Burnet, *History*, iv, 190.

17 Clarke, *Life*, ii, 140.

18 Angus McIntyre, 'The College, King James II and the Revolution of 1687–88', *Magdalen College and the Crown: Essays for the Tercentenary of the Restoration of the College, 1688*, eds L. Brockliss, G. Harris and A. McIntyre (Oxford, 1988), p. 46. Quoting Magdalen College MS 432.

19 *An impartial relation of the whole proceedings against St Mary Magdalen College*, 1688. Bonrepos, a French envoy to England who was present at Oxford, noted that James 's'est mis dans un fureur extraordinaire et transporte de colere', PRO 31/3/172, Bonrepos to Seignelay, 4/14 Sept. 1687.

20 Bodleian Ballard MSS 21, fo. 10. Thomas Sykes to Arthur Charlett, 7 Sept. 1687. Bonrepos reported on 4 September that James had told the Magdalen Fellows that he would make them feel the weight of a king's hand. He thought that James's behaviour towards them was detrimental to his cause. PRO 31/3/172.

21 Bodleian MSS Smith 141, fo. 21. A Magdalen Fellow wrote to a relative on 18 September that James had said 'or else you must expect to feel the heavy hand of an angry king'. McIntyre, p. 31. Quoting Magdalen MSS 421.

22 Bodleian MSS Smith 141, fo. 21. The threat of military involvement was not idle. When the commissioners revisited the college on 15 November they were accompanied by three troops of horse. Ibid., fo. 25.

23 Morrice MSS Q, p. 170.

24 Mark Goldie, 'James II and the Dissenters' revenge: the commission of enquiry of 1688', *Historical Research*, vol. lxvi (1993), 53–88.

25 According to Roger Morrice, Butler was 'very considerable for his interest. He often attends upon his Majesty and seems to be as much in favour with him as any one subject whatsoever and to be privy to all his counsels and to have a great influence upon them. Sir Nicholas does understand his Majesty very well and can feel his pulse.' Morrice MSS, p. 169.

26 Mark Knights, 'A City revolution: The remodelling of the London livery companies in the 1680s', *English Historical Review*, vol. cxii (1998), 1158.

27 Bodleian Rawlinson MSS A 139b, fo. 184.

28 *Calendar of State Papers Domestic 1687–9*, p. 118.

29 Morrice MSS Q, p. 239 (2). The passage is repeated in pp. 243–4.

30 For a summary of views up to 1988, see W. A. Speck, *Reluctant Revolutionaries* (Oxford, 1988), pp.131–2. Two recent investigations continue the debate. M. J. Short concludes that they were good: 'The corporation of Hull and the government of James II', *Historical Research*, vol. lxxi (1998), 172–95 . By contrast, Paul D. Halliday concludes that 'James' effort in 1687–88 to reshape the electorate in order to gain a Parliament ready to grant religious toleration ... would not have worked. We know this because it did not work!', *Dismembering the Body Politic: Partisan politics in England's towns, 1650–1730* (Cambridge, 1998), p. 239.

31 Bodleian Rawlinson MSS A 139b, fo. 178. For *Fagel's Letter to James Stewart* 'giving an account of the Prince and Princess of Orange's thoughts concerning the repeal of the Test and Penal Laws' see below, p. 138.

32 Bodleian Rawlinson MSS A 139b, fo. 178. Apparently such counter-propaganda was produced, for in September the regulators reported 'that the books that have been dispersed have had very good effect'. Ibid., fo. 186.

33 Not dated, but after June, as one memorandum requires the agents 'to take care to make all persons understand that the late proceedings against the Bishops were necessary to support his Majesty's Declaration for Liberty of Conscience, which the King will always maintain, as likewise his prerogative on which it is founded'.

34 *The Autobiography of Sir John Bramston*, ed. Lord Braybrooke (London, 1845), p. 356.

35 Cumbria Archives Service, Kendal; Rydal MSS 3238, Henry Fleming to Sir Daniel Fleming, 29 July 1688.

36 Algemeen Rijksarchief, The Hague, States General 591 (2), James II to the States General, 11 June 1688.

37 BL Add. MSS 9341, fo. 53.

38 National Library of Wales, Ottley MSS 1467.

39 PRO 30/53/8, fo. 64, anon. to Lord Herbert, 16 June 1688.

40 Morrice MSS Q, p. 264.

41 Bodleian Tanner MS 28, fo. 39. 'This is the sum of what past, as far as the Bps could recollect it.' James himself recalled that he also told them 'that the seditious preachings of the Puritans in the year [16]40 was not of so ill consequence as this, that they had raised a devil they could not lay'. Clarke, ii, 155.

42 *Publications of the Surtees Society*, vol. xlvii (1865), 147.

43 Bodleian Tanner MSS 28, fo. 50.

44 *The Life and Times of Anthony Wood*, ed. Andrew Clark (Oxford, 1894), iii, 267.

45 Singer, ii, 177.

46 *An Answer to a Letter to a Dissenter* (1687), 3.

47 J. P. Kenyon, *The Stuart Constitution* (2nd edition, London, 1986), p. 410.

48 Clarke, *Life*, ii, 163.

49 Morrice MSS Q, p. 258.

50 *The Ellis Correspondence*, ed. G. A. Ellis (London, 1829), ii, 109.

51 *The Autobiography of Sir John Bramston*, p. 312.

52 Bodleian Rawlinson MSS A 139b, fo. 186.

Chapter Four

The Revolution

Until late September 1688 James had refused to look facts in the face, totally disbelieving reports that his son-in-law was preparing to invade England. This had been obvious to other observers for some time. As early as May, the comte d'Avaux, Louis XIV's ambassador at The Hague, reported preparations by the Secretary of the Amsterdam Admiralty to equip twelve ships to be ready to sail, which could only be intended against England.[1] To some extent James was let down by his own ambassador to the Dutch Republic, the marquis d'Albeville, who was not as well informed as his French counterpart. It was not until the third week in September that d'Albeville became aware that 'their goeing for England is no more a secret in these parts'.[2] At the same time James seems to have been in denial, not wanting to believe that his own family could be so treacherous. On 25 August, the very experienced and astute French diplomat Usson de Bonrepos had an audience with James and warned him of his danger, urging him to make contingent plans to meet it. The comte d'Adda, the papal envoy, told James on 31 August of William's intentions. Yet it was not until 10 September that Barillon informed Louis XIV that the English king began to be persuaded that the Prince of Orange had formed a design to make a descent upon England. And it was not until 24 September that he was finally convinced that the Dutch really were going to invade.

This realisation led him to recall the writs for a new parliament which had been issued on 18 September. Not only did he call off the general election, he threw the whole electoral machinery into reverse. Thus Anglican tories were reinstated as deputy lieutenants of the county militias and justices of the peace, while the Catholics and dissenters who had replaced them were ousted. 'His Majesty by this one gracious act has done a great work', Lord Bath informed Lord Sunderland from Cornwall, 'having settled the minds of the people beyond expectation.'[3] The king also restored the charter to the city of London which had been taken from it in the 'tory reaction' of the early 1680s. Ever since 1683 the capital had been governed by men appointed by the Crown. No elections had been held and no Common Council had sat. The city, with its long history of independence from the Crown, was reduced to a royal pocket borough. Now the right of election was restored to the livery companies and London became virtually autonomous again. Roger Morrice saw these reversals of policy as an attempt to 'rectifie the fundamental mistake in laying aside the Tories'.[4]

James's reversal of his tactics since the dissolution of parliament the previous summer went much further in that direction. On 24 September he invited nine bishops, including the archbishop of Canterbury and three others of the seven he had prosecuted for seditious libel, to meet him. Sancroft and his episcopal colleagues drew up a list of ten recommendations which they presented to the king on 3 October. The first was 'that he would please to put the management of the government into the hands of such as were legally quallifyed for it', i.e. communicating Anglicans. Since the earl of Sunderland had publicly announced his conversion to Catholicism that summer, the implementation of this would purge the government of one who, until the scare of the imminent invasion, had been the king's most important adviser. But James rather blamed Sunderland for the scrape he was in, and dismissed him on 27 October. Once again Godolphin emerged from the shadows to play a crucial role in the rehabilitation of the tories. He it was who liaised with the bishops, encouraging them to submit their recommendations, since, as he informed the bishop of Ely, 'whatever now was fit to be askt by us we might have it granted, at least by degrees'.[5]

The bishops' second recommendation was that the commission for ecclesiastical causes should be annulled. This had already been adjourned from August until December, apparently on Sunderland's advice. It had been engaged on an investigation of the clergy who had refused to read the Declaration of Indulgence from their pulpits, a highly divisive enquiry which had led the bishop of Rochester to resign from it. James suspended the commission, and for good measure restored the bishop of London to his spiritual functions from which he had been deprived by the commissioners.

The third recommendation presented to the king was that he should issue no dispensations to men who were not legally qualified. It also urged him to 'restore Magdalen College to the President and ancient Fellows'.

They were duly reinstated. Other recommendations put to the king were 'that he would please to restore the charters to other corporations as he had been pleased to do in London' and 'that he would be pleased to call a Parliament where the Act of Uniformity might be settled and provision made for a due liberty of conscience'. James was also asked 'to inhibit the four foreign Bishops who style themselves Vicars Apostolical from further invading the Ecclesiastical Jurisdiction which is by law vested in the Bishops of this Church'. He was also urged to fill the archbishopric of York, which had been vacant for some time, and concerning which some fears had been expressed that the king designed to appoint a Catholic to it. Finally they asked James to allow them to try to convince him to return to the Anglican Church. While he was prepared to yield immediately some concessions, and to consider others, this last was out of the question.[6]

James's sincerity in making these concessions is questionable. He had previously projected himself as a resolute monarch who would not yield to the importunities of his subjects. This had earned him the reputation of 'a prince who is famous [over all Europe] for being firm and steady to his word and thereby hath ... acquired and deserved the title James the Just'.[7] Now his caving in to the demands of men, four of whom he had brought to trial only a few months before, seemed to be a sign of weakness. He probably yielded to them in order to wrongfoot the Prince of Orange, since he conceded many of the grievances that had made his subjects turn to William to seek redress. 'Nothing seems wanting but a free parliament', observed a newsletter writer, 'and then I can't see what the Prince will do.'[8] Having 'done in a manner all that they could wish', on 16 October James 'earnestly pressed' the bishops to 'declare an abhorrence of the invasion itself', but to his consternation they refused.[9]

James was further mortified by the Prince of Orange's Declaration, which cast doubts on the legitimacy of the Prince of Wales. William undertook to conduct an inquiry into the circumstances of the birth of a son to Mary of Modena in June, thus feeding the fantasy that a supposititious child had been introduced into the royal bedchamber in a warming pan. He also asserted that many of the nobility had invited him to come to England to rescue them from popery and arbitrary power. James resolved to tackle both these claims head on.

On 22 October the king held an extraordinary meeting of peers, bishops, judges, the Lord Mayor and the aldermen of London in the council chamber to hear evidence relating to the birth of the Prince of Wales. The king had summoned them, he told them when they met, because he was expecting the Prince of Orange to invade, and was determined to 'go in person against him', which could lead to his death. He did not want there to be any uncertainty about the succession should he die. 'The malicious endeavours of my enemies have so poisoned the minds of some of my subjects', he declared, 'that by the reports I have from all hands, I have reason to believe that very many do not think this son, with which God hath blessed me, to be mine but a supposed child. But I may say that by particular Providence, scarce any Prince was ever born where there were so many persons present.' Forty witnesses to the birth swore on oath that the queen had been delivered of a son. Their depositions were enrolled in Chancery and published by authority.[10]

On 2 November the archbishop of Canterbury and four of his episcopal colleagues were summoned to an audience. They found the earl of Middleton there, clutching a copy of the Prince of Orange's Declaration. The king asked him to read out the passage claiming that members of the nobility had invited him over. The previous day James had asked the bishop of London whether he was included in their number. Compton had denied it, which was a lie as he was one of the seven who invited the Prince. Now James asked the five bishops who attended the audience, who included Compton, whether the prince's claim was false. The archbishop insisted that it must be, since 'he did not know nor could believe that any of his brethren the Bishops had given the Prince any such invitation'.[11] Compton equivocated by saying that he had given his answer the day before. The others swore their innocence. James then twice asked them to publish a denial and an abhorrence of the prince's design, but they said nothing, and so the audience came to an end.

On 6 November, the day after William's landing in Torbay, the king again saw four of the bishops at Whitehall. Two who had not been present at the previous meeting now denied their complicity in the invitation. James assured them he had no suspicions of them, but then asked, 'where is the paper I desired you to draw up and bring me?' When they told him they had not brought one, he insisted that they had promised one. They replied that they could not repudiate claims made in the Declaration, which James held in his hands, until it was proved to be the prince's. The king insisted it was authentic. Sancroft then pointed out that he, along with six other bishops, had suffered for meddling in matters of state.

James replied that he thought their trial was 'a matter quite out of the way. I thought this had all bin forgotten.' 'As for what you say that 'tis hazardous to meddle in matters of state', he continued, showing he had not really changed his ways, 'that is true when I do not call you to it. But I may ask counsel or assistance of any as I now do of you, and then there can be no danger.' Again he insisted that they had promised a paper abhorring the invasion, and asked Lord Preston, who was present, to confirm this, which he did. Sancroft then claimed there were too few bishops to make a general abhorrence for the whole episcopate, which James countered by denying there was time to send to remote sees like Carlisle or Exeter, and that if those at the audience would subscribe, then he would undertake to get further signatures. The bishops then pointed out that temporal lords were also implicated in the invitation, and should therefore be invited to join them. James insisted that it would be more for his service for them to do it, since they had 'a greater interest with the people'. They replied 'that in matters of this nature belonging to civil government, and the affairs of war and peace, it was most probable the nobility would have a far greater influence on the nation'.

James, clearly exasperated with them, then insisted that 'this is the method I have proposed. I am your King. I am Judge of what is best for me. I will go my own way. I desire your assistance in it.' Put on the spot, the bishops were prepared to accept publication of their innocence, provided James would undertake to publish it. He replied, 'no, if I should publish it the people would not believe me'. Upon their protestations that the word of a king was sacred, and that the people were bound to believe it, he observed that 'they that could believe me guilty of a false son, what will they not believe of me?' He then insisted that the bishops should comply with his demands, but they would only undertake to support him in parliament. Then he ended the audience by saying, 'my Lords that is a business of more time. What I ask now I think of present concern to my affairs. But this is the last time. I will argue no further. If you will not assist me as I desire I must stand upon my own legs, and trust to my self and my own arms.'[12]

James thus hazarded everything on the outcome of the contest between himself and the Prince of Orange. If he won, then as he admitted, he would be 'absolute master to doe what he pleased'.[13] It seems certain that his autocratic temperament, as displayed in the audiences with the bishops, would not be satisfied with the role of a limited monarch. If he lost, then as he told the French ambassador, he would leave the country rather than be beholden to his son-in-law.[14]

James made contingent plans for both eventualities. To put himself into a position to win, he deployed the fleet to intercept the prince, and mobilised 40,000 troops to defend him against attack. Some were brought to England from Ireland and Scotland to reinforce the army camped on Hounslow Heath, bringing it up to a force of about 25,000 men. The king hoped these would be sufficient to defeat the Prince of Orange. But in case he lost, he arranged to send his wife and infant son to France, where he intended to join them.

Victory, rather than defeat, in his view depended on the continued support of divine Providence. Its assistance was invoked in special prayers which James ordered to be used in all churches imploring God to 'save and protect him' and to 'give thy holy Angels charge over him'.[15] It seemed ironic to his Anglican subjects that they were being required to pray for the safety of a Catholic king who threatened that of their church. Initially this intercession seemed to work when the first Dutch invasion attempt in mid-October was driven back by violent storms. This put a stop to the restoration of borough charters. 'This is very instructive to let us know that the Restauration proceeds not from inclination but from necessity', noted Roger Morrice, 'and that the Court will change their Councils if the present distresses were over.'[16] James also took comfort from the fact that the westerly gales pinned the Dutch in their home ports. 'I see God Almighty continues his Protection to me', he wrote to the earl of Dartmouth on 20 October, 'by bringing the wind westerly again.'[17] Late in October, however, the 'Protestant wind' blew from the east, allowing the Dutch taskforce to sail down the English channel to Torbay where William landed on 5 November.

James's initial reaction to the news was to stay in London and oblige the prince to advance to the capital. This appeared to the king to give him the military advantage. It seems clear that he intended to engage the Dutch army in battle. Others were anxious to avoid bloodshed. A number of bishops and peers presented a petition to James urging him to call a free parliament to avert a conflict. 'What you ask of me', he told them, 'I most passionately desire: and I promise you, upon the faith of a King, that I will have a parliament and such a one as you ask for, as soon as ever the Prince of Orange has quitted this realm; for how is it possible a Parliament should be free in all its circumstances as you petition for, whilst an enemy is in the Kingdom, and can make a return of near an hundred voices?'[18]

Since William had not advanced immediately towards London, but stayed in Exeter to refresh his troops and receive recruits, James decided to go down to Salisbury to intercept him. A newsletter reported that the king 'declared that he went with a full resolution to give the enemy battle, and affirmed his former sentiment that if it did please God to give him success he would divide the estates of the rebels among the officers and soldiers of his army and not give the least to any courtiers'.[19] He does not appear to have considered that the invading troops were superior to his own army, though some recent estimates have claimed that William's were more numerous. Where previous calculations credited William with 14,000 men to the king's 25,000 it has been asserted that the prince had almost as many if not more troops at his disposal than did James.[20] These revised estimates, however, have not been generally accepted.[21] The most reliable calculation is that of the contemporary John Whittle, a chaplain who accompanied the Dutch taskforce and witnessed the review of his troops by the Prince of Orange when they disembarked at Brixham. 'The Number of all his Forces and Souldiers', he recorded '[was] about fifteen thousand four hundred and odd men.'[22]

The relative strengths of the two armies were never put to the test, as within four days of arriving in Salisbury James decided to return to London. His decision was taken while he was suffering from the debilitating effects of a severe nosebleed. This is sometimes diagnosed by historians as a psychosomatic disorder. But, while the king was also exhibiting symptoms of irrationality and even of derangement during the closing weeks of 1688, the illness seems to have been physical enough to alarm observers into thinking he had a brain tumour. 'Tis generally thought that his Majesty is very ill', a newsletter reported in December, 'of an imposthume which is inward from his nose and up into his head.'[23] How far he was in his right mind when he resolved to return to the capital can therefore be doubted. In so far as it was a rational decision, however, it appears to have been based on his estimate not of the size of William's army but of the extent of disloyalty in his own, especially in the officer corps. The day after it was taken, a number of his high command, including John Churchill, the future duke of Marlborough, deserted to the Prince of Orange. Typically James later attributed his nosebleed to Providence, since if he had not been ill he would have advanced towards the prince's lines and been delivered up to William as a captive by the arch-deserter Churchill.

Upon his return to London on 26 November he learned that his daughter Anne had also deserted him and gone to Nottingham accompanied by Sarah Churchill, John's wife, and the bishop of London. This blow was even more bitter than the treachery of his high command. Princess Anne was sure of a good reception at Nottingham, since supporters of the Prince of Orange led by the earl of Devonshire had taken control of it on 20 November. Two days later the northern capital of York was seized by Orangists led by the earl of Danby. Uprisings in other parts of the provinces were under way or about to break out. The aims of the insurgents were varied. Some, especially those who accompanied William of Orange on his expedition, hoped, like the prince, that he would somehow replace James on the throne. Others, such as those who went along with Danby in Yorkshire, were bent on bringing the king to his senses. What united the participants behind William was his demand for a free parliament.

On 27 November, James invited all the peers in London to advise him how to proceed. About forty attended the meeting. The earl of Rochester, now reinstated as a leading adviser, urged him to call parliament as 'the only remedy in our present circumstances'.[24] James had earlier rejected this advice as being inappropriate during an invasion, but now accepted it and asked the peers how it could be implemented in the state of emergency.

> The Lords were all unanimous in saying the meeting of a parliament might be practicable if his Majesty pleased to enter into a treaty with the Prince of Orange, and would make such concessions as the elections might be free, the desisting from the exercising the dispensing power, the giving a general pardon that all the Lords who are now with the Prince of Orange and who are up in the other counties and all the gentlemen who are engaged might have free liberty to be chosen and to come to parliament as if these stirs had never been.[25]

James asked for time to consider these proposals, but the next day declared that a parliament should meet on 15 January. Writs were consequently issued for a general election. He also agreed to send three peers as emissaries to the Prince of Orange. But his heart was in none of these arrangements. As he told the peers at their meeting, 'it would appear that the Prince of Orange came for the crown, whatever he pretended; but that he would not see himself deposed; that he had read the story of Richard

II'.[26] James also told the French ambassador that he had gone along with them just to buy time while he sent his wife and son to France.

James himself was undecided what action to take. It seems he did not intend to meet the parliament summoned for 15 January, since it would only demand measures which he was not prepared to take, such as the dismissal of all Catholics from his service. Such limitations on the royal prerogative did not appeal to him. He toyed with the idea of going to Scotland, which the duke of Hamilton encouraged, or to Ireland, which Tyrconnel recommended. In the event he decided to join the queen and the Prince of Wales in France. After an abortive attempt to get them out of the country on 8 December, his wife and infant son successfully crossed the Channel on 10 December. James informed the earl of Feversham, whom he had left in command of the army on Salisbury plain, that he had resolved to follow them. 'If I could have relied upon all my troops', he lamented, 'I might not have been put to this extremity I am in, and would at least have had one blow for it.'[27] He also wrote to the earl of Dartmouth, who commanded the fleet, to inform him that he had 'resolved to withdraw till this violent storm is over'.[28] On the night of 10 December the earl of Ailesbury waited on the king and begged him not to go. James asked what alternative there was after he had been deserted by his daughter and Churchill. Ailesbury replied that he could go to Nottingham and confront Anne, or, failing that, go to York and challenge Danby, 'with his broomsticks and whishtail militia ... who will all run away. And then, Sir, secure Berwick and march into Scotland, and ... that kingdom will be entirely yours'.[29] Ailesbury's attempt to put some spirit into James was of no avail, however, for early the following morning the king left London for France. He took the great seal of England with him, to abort the elections then in progress, and threw it into the Thames as he crossed the river to Lambeth. There, Sir Edward Hales was waiting for him with horses. They rode to Elmley Ferry where they boarded a customs boat to set sail for France.

Unfortunately the boat ran aground at Sheppey and was boarded by seamen from Faversham searching for Sir Edward Hales. Not knowing they had also apprehended the king they took him for what they were pleased to call an 'old rogue, ugly, lean-jaw'd hatchet-fac't Jesuite, popish dog, etc'.[30] On 12 December they conveyed him to the Queen's Arms in Faversham, where they learned who he was and permitted him to write a letter to the earl of Winchilsea. 'I am just now come in here having been last night seas'd by some of this town', James wrote. 'I desire you would come hither to me ... that I might advise with you concerning my safety.'[31] While he was waiting for Winchilsea to arrive he borrowed a Bible and read aloud passages which indicate his mental state. Thus he quoted 1 Maccabees xi 10, 'I repent that I gave my daughter to him, for he sought to slay me', which documented his view of the Prince of Orange. James undoubtedly believed that he was in imminent danger of death if he fell into William's hands. He also said that 'he wd forsake sceptre and crowns and all this world's glory for Xt's sake, and he had yt inward peace and cofort wch he wd not exchange for all ye interest of ye earth'. 'If he lost his temporal crown, he doubted not, but ye loss wd bring him to an eternal and incorruptible crown.'[32] He was clearly anticipating eagerly the contemplative life he was to lead in France.

When Winchilsea arrived, the earl persuaded the seamen to allow James to move to a private house, though they insisted on mounting guard there to prevent his escaping. One of them went up to London with the news that the king was at Faversham. In his absence a group of peers had taken upon themselves the role of government and met in the Guildhall. The seaman was summoned into their presence, where his intelligence stunned the assembled peers. Lord Ailesbury broke the silence by moving that James should be invited back to the capital. The earl was then nominated along with Secretary of State Middleton, the earl of Feversham and the treasurer of the household to go down to Faversham to accompany the king to London. When they got there on 14 December Lord Winchilsea led them to the house where James was lodged. Ailesbury recalled the moment when he first saw the king, who was 'sitting in a great chair, his hat on, and his beard much grown, and resembled the picture of his royal father at the pretended high Court of Justice'.[33] As they made their way back to London they were met by vast crowds who greeted the king with great enthusiasm. 'From St George's Southwark, to Whitehall, a long march, there was scarce room for the coaches to pass through, and the balconies and windows besides were thronged with loud acclamations beyond whatever was heard of', recalled Ailesbury. 'In fine the joy was so great and general, that if there had been any foreigners in the streets and subjects to a despotic King or Commonwealth whose subjects more fears than loves their superiors, they would imagine that they had been all mad.'[34] The jubilation was extraordinary given the aversion to popery which the London crowds customarily displayed during James's reign. The king himself took it as a sign that he was genuinely popular among the mass of his subjects. This was a delusion which was to mislead him into thinking that he would be welcomed back in England when he attempted to return there via Ireland after the Revolution. The demonstrations in London displayed not affection for the king but relief that the restoration of normal government might also restore law and order. Ever since his departure there had been a breakdown of law and order coupled with wild rumours that Irish soldiers, demobilised when Feversham disbanded the army, were on the rampage, pillaging, raping and killing Protestants. The return of the king was a great relief, promising to end the anarchy.

Indeed, for a brief interval it seemed that normal government had been resumed. James even presided over a meeting of the Privy Council. It resolved to direct lords lieutenant of counties to suppress disorderly and riotous gatherings. William, however, was determined that this state of affairs should not continue. He had been delighted to learn that the king had fled, and made his way towards London. But he was chagrined to discover that James had not made good his escape, and had despatched a messenger to Faversham to persuade him not to return to the capital but to retire to Rochester. The message had not got through. Instead, James sent Feversham to the prince to inform him that he had been rescued from his plight. William demonstrated his displeasure by arresting Feversham on the specious grounds that he had acted without warrant when he disbanded his troops. James was shocked by this arbitrary action, and even more so when William sent Dutch soldiers to replace the English guards at St James's, Somerset House and Whitehall. The final indignity was to be awoken between one and two o'clock in the morning of 17 December to give audience to three peers sent by the prince: Delamere, Halifax and Shrewsbury. They informed James that William desired him to move to Ham House, up the Thames near Richmond. The king responded that he would rather go to Rochester. The three emissaries took this request to the prince and returned at eight o'clock with his assent to it. At eleven o'clock James went on board a barge which conveyed him down the river to Gravesend. It was quite obvious that Rochester was intended as a temporary stopping place on his way to France. 'If I do not retire', the king told Ailesbury, 'I shall certainly be sent to the Tower, and no King ever went out of that place but to his grave.'[35] In the early hours of 23 December James was rowed to a yacht waiting for him in Queenborough and sailed in it to France.

Before leaving Rochester, James published his reasons for withdrawing himself a second time. He adduced the arrest of Feversham by William 'against the practice and law of nations', posting Dutch guards in royal posts at Whitehall 'without advertising me in the least manner of it', and sending orders at one o'clock in the morning for him to be out of his own palace before noon. 'After all this how could I hope to be safe, so long as I was in the power of one who had not only done this to me, and invaded my kingdoms without any just occasion given him for it, but that did by his first Declaration lay the greatest aspersion upon me that malice could invent in that clause of it which concerns my son? ... What had I then to expect from one who by all arts hath taken such pains to make me appear as black as hell to my own people as well as to the world besides?' This had led to the defections in the army as well as in the nation. 'I was born free', the king concluded, 'and desire to continue so; and tho' I have ventured my life very frankly, on several occasions, for the good and honour of my country, and am as free to do it again (and which I shall yet do, as old as I am, to redeem it from the slavery it is like to fall under); yet I think it not convenient to expose my self to be secured, as not to be at liberty to effect it; and for that reason to withdraw, but so as to be within call whenever the nation's eyes shall be opened.'[36]

The nation's eyes were more focused on the problem of how to fill the throne left void by James's departure than to recall him to it. On 24 December a number of peers met to discuss the situation. Lord Paget moved that James's withdrawal was an abdication, and that his daughter Mary should be declared queen. Although the bishop of London seconded the proposal, the peers instead resolved to address William of Orange to take over the administration of the government, and to issue writs for a Convention to meet on 22 January. After consulting other interested parties, including former members of Charles II's parliaments and the mayor, aldermen and councillors of London, William agreed. Elections were duly held and the Convention assembled. A letter from William was read out to the members warning them that 'next to the danger of unseasonable divisions amongst yourselves, nothing can be so fatal as too great delay in your consultations'. It took three weeks for the Houses to agree that the throne was vacant, that the crown should be offered to William and Mary, and that they should be asked to accept a Declaration of Rights which enumerated actions by James which were declared to be illegal.

Although this in hindsight appears to have been accomplished with despatch, at the time it seemed to have been protracted by 'unseasonable divisions', especially in the Lords. These have been attributed to diehard supporters of James determined to hold out for him. Although nobody was prepared to invite him back, there were those who maintained that a vacancy of the throne was a constitutional impossibility in a hereditary monarchy. If the king was physically incapable of governing, either through illness or absence, then a regency was the only institution for the continuance of government. While some who went along with this proposal were undoubtedly supporters of James, or Jacobites, the notion that Jacobitism was a significant element in the Convention is unsustainable. As early as 29 January the Commons had resolved 'that it hath been found, by experience, to be inconsistent with the safety and welfare of this Protestant kingdom to be governed by a Popish Prince'. On 7 February the Lords agreed without a division that 'no Papist may succeed' to the crown 'nor any person that hath made or shall make a profession of being a Papist'. These resolutions set aside the claims of James altogether and even of his infant should he declare himself a Catholic. They were to be the biggest single impediment to a Stuart restoration.

The objections to the notion that the throne was vacant, and the support for a regency, came not just from Jacobites but from tories such as the earls of Nottingham and Rochester, whose loyalties lay with the Church of England more than with the exiled king. They had genuine legal scruples about the methods which the Convention adopted to fill the vacuum left by his departure. Other tories, such as the earl of Danby, were more inclined to offer the crown to Mary as queen, but not to make William king. It took William's own indication that he would return to the Netherlands if he were not offered the crown too to concentrate minds wonderfully.

The Declaration of Rights, which the Convention offered to William and Mary on 13 February, provided for the unique dual monarchy of the pair, in which he was to be the sole executive. The Declaration has been construed by some historians as a whig document. But the list of charges against the exiled king reflected far more tory disapproval of his actions than it did whig. Thus it claimed that he had endeavoured to extirpate the Protestant religion and the laws and liberties of England by, *inter alia*, 'committing and prosecuting diverse worthy Prelates for humbly petitioning to be excused from concurring to the said assumed power'. The seven bishops were not whig but tory heroes. The commission for ecclesiastical causes, the suspension of the bishop of London and the ejection of the Fellows of Magdalen College, all similarly condemned, were causes much more dear to tories than to whigs. The strength of the tories in the Convention became clear when it went on to discuss the religious settlement. Attempts to alter the liturgy of the Church of England to comprehend Presbyterians came to naught. Instead, dissenters had to be content with a Toleration Act which gave them far less than James's Declarations of Indulgence. Thus the Corporation and Test Acts were specifically upheld by it. James had tested the twin loyalties of the tories to church and king until they had to make a choice. In the Glorious Revolution most demonstrated that their first loyalty lay with the Church of England.

Notes and references

1 *Négociations de Monsieur le comte d'Avaux en Hollande depuis 1684 jusqu'en 1688* (6 vols, Paris, 1752–3), vi, 146–7.

2 BL Add. MSS 41816, fo. 209.

3 *Calendar of State Papers Domestic 1687–9*, p. 286.

4 Morrice MSS Q, p. 296.

5 Bodleian Tanner MSS 28, fo. 185.

6 Bodleian Tanner MSS 28, fo. 87. A version differing in some respects was printed in *An account of the proposals of the archbishop of Canterbury with some other bishops to his majesty in a letter to M. B. Esq* (1688). Thus the first recommendation begins: 'the Bishops thought fit to represent in general to his Majesty, that it was necessary for him to restore all things to the state in which he found them when he came to the Crown'. This expression is not in Sancroft's version, though it undoubtedly sums up his aspirations.

7 Bodleian Tanner MSS 31, fo. 250, Bishop of Norwich to Sancroft, 29 June 1686.

8 BL Add. MSS 34487, fo. 30, newsletter 4 Oct. 1688.

9 Clarke, *Life*, ii, 190.

10 *Proceedings in the Council Chamber 22 October 1688*, a 40-page pamphlet 'published by his Majesty's special command'.

11 Bodleian Tanner MSS 28, fo. 220.

12 Bodleian Tanner MSS 28, fos 233–7, 'The Bp of Rochester's Relation'.

13 Clarke, *Life*, ii, 211.

14 Barillon to Louis XIV, 20/30 Sept. 1688.

15 J. Gutch, *Collectanea Curiosa* (2 vols, Oxford, 1781), i, 417.

16 Morrice MSS Q, fo. 308.

17 HMC *Dartmouth*, i, 169.

18 The king's reply to the petition was published with an imprimatur dated 20 November 1688. The king's promise of a parliament after the Dutch had withdrawn was characterised by Orangists as 'such a free Parliament as they were like to have had before the Prince came hither, shuffl'd, cut and pack't by Mr Brent and his missionaries', i.e. the regulators of corporations. *A Modest Vindication of the Petition of the Lords Spiritual and Temporal for the calling of a free Parliament* (Exeter, 21 November 1688).

19 BL Add. MSS 34487, fo. 37, London, 20 November 1688.

20 Jonathan Israel, 'The Dutch role in the Glorious Revolution', *The Anglo-Dutch Moment: Essays on the Glorious Revolution and its world impact*, ed. J. Israel (Cambridge, 1991), p. 106, where the invading army is estimated to have been 21,000 strong. Eveline Cruickshanks, *The Glorious Revolution* (London, 2000) gives an even higher estimate.

21 See Stephen Saunders Webb, *Lord Churchill's Coup: The Anglo-American empire and the Glorious Revolution reconsidered* (London, 1995), p. 141.

22 *An Exact Diary of the Late Expedition of his illustrious Highness the Prince of Orange* (1689), p. 40.

23 BL Add. MSS 34487, fo. 50. It was observed when James was at Salisbury that he 'bleeds upon every occasion at the nose and mouth and much purulent matter comes out'. BL Egerton MSS 2621, fo. 67.

24 Singer, ii, 209.

25 Bodleian Carte MSS 130, fo. 311, anon. to marquis of Worcester, 29 November 1688.

26 Singer, ii, 211.

27 BL Add. MSS 32095, fo. 297.

28 HMC *Dartmouth*, i, 226.

29 *Memoirs of Ailesbury*, i, 195–6. Ailesbury claimed that Danby later admitted that if James had gone to York he would have submitted to him and craved his pardon.

30 *Notes and Queries*, 3rd series (1864), v, 391.

31 BL Add. MSS 32095, fo. 298.

32 *Notes and Queries*, p. 393.

33 *Memoirs of Ailesbury*, i, 209.

34 Ibid., p. 215.

35 Ibid., p. 224.

36 *His Majesties Reasons for withdrawing himself from Rochester, writ with his own hand, and ordered by him to be published*. Rochester, 22 December 1688. A riposte appeared which printed the broadside with comments on some of its claims. Thus the commentator glossed the claim made by James that William had no just occasion for his invasion with the observation 'but my going about to ruin the established government of the nation and the Protestant religion'. *The King's Reasons (with some reflections upon them)*.

Chapter Five

James VII

James was proclaimed king in Edinburgh on 10 February 1685. The militia companies were drawn up at the Cross where they were joined by the Chancellor, James Drummond, earl of Perth, the Treasurer, William Douglas, duke of Queensberry, other officers and noblemen, the Privy Council, the judges, the magistrates and the whole town council. The Chancellor, 'weeping, declared James duke of Albany the only undoubted and lawful King of this realme, under the name of James the 7th'. It was made clear when the event was reported that Perth had made a declaration not a proclamation, to avoid any implication that 'the people had any hand in giving him power'.[1] As in England, James's accession to the throne of Scotland was popularly acclaimed. 'Never King succeeded to a throne more with the love and esteem of his subjects than your Majesty', observed the earl of Balcarres.[2]

As duke of York and Albany, James had felt to be more among friends in Scotland, when he went into exile there during the Exclusion crisis, than he had in England. The Scots seemed much more amenable to his idea of kingship than were the English. This persuaded him that he would be more of a king as James VII of Scotland than as James II of England. He soon demonstrated this conviction by not consulting the secret committee of the Scottish Privy Council, which under Charles II had enjoyed more autonomy, before issuing instructions to them. As one informed observer noted, 'the active genius of our present King is more for hastie dispatch of business, and inclines more to rule alone then his brother (who affected ease) did'.[3]

James hoped that getting off to a good start north of the border would set an example in the southern kingdom. He therefore got the Scottish parliament to meet on 23 April, before the English met, 'to distinguish the confidence he had in the Scotch Nobility and Gentry who had stuck so close to him in his adversitie'.[4]

The duke of Queensberry, who presided over their session as commissioner, encouraged the Scottish MPs to give a lead to the king's other dominions. They obliged by passing a list of Acts which James had communicated to them through the Lords of the Articles, the body which channelled legislation through the Edinburgh parliament. They made as generous a financial settlement as they could, annexing the excise to the Crown in perpetuity and voting other revenues calculated to yield £60,000 a year.

James had asked the Lords 'to endeavour the obtaining an Act asserting our prerogative over all persons and in all cases in most ample form'.[5] His 'sacred, supreme and absolute power' as king of Scotland was duly affirmed in the preamble to the Excise Act. After counting their blessings for the beneficial effects of two thousand years of national history 'in the unaltered form of our monarchical government', it went on to attribute them first to Divine Mercy and then 'to the sacred race of our Glorious Kings and to that solid, absolute authority wherewith they were invested by the first and fundamental law of our monarchy'. It then declared the parliament's abhorrence of 'all principles and positions which are contrary or derogatory to the King's sacred, supreme, sovereign, absolute power and authority'. The preamble concluded by renewing 'the hearty and sincere offer of their lives and fortunes to assist, support, defend and maintain King James the seventh ... against all mortals'.[6] 'I see how well you and the parliament have begun', James congratulated Queensberry on 3 May, 'which will be a very good presedent to the English one.'[7]

His request for severity against those who attended field conventicles was answered by an Act making attendance a capital offence. The death penalty was even to be imposed on those who harboured field conventiclers. Macaulay described this as 'the most sanguinary law that has ever been enacted in our island against Protestant Nonconformists'.[8] It certainly seems at odds with James's protestations of a belief in religious toleration. But this was limited, like that of his brother's commitment to liberty for tender consciences in the Declaration of Breda, to those who 'did not disturb the peace of the kingdom'. The Covenanters, against whom the laws were principally directed, most certainly did disturb the peace, for they had openly declared war against the regime. Even modern democracies find they have to curtail the rights of their citizens in order to deal with terrorists.

This justifies, if it does not totally excuse, the conduct of men like John Graham of Claverhouse, who were in charge of the execution of the laws against Covenanters. 'Clavers', as he was known, was a man after James's own heart. A soldier by profession, he had been in the service of the Prince of Orange until 1678, when William recommended him to his father-in-law. Claverhouse was a rough, short-tempered man of action, the Scottish equivalent of Tyrconnel. James was much more at his ease with such men than with the cultured courtiers and career politicians whom he had to deal with. When Claverhouse entered his service he was involved in the military suppression of the field conventicles, and was present at the battle of Bothwell Bridge. While James was in Scotland he enjoyed the duke's patronage and protection. After he returned to England, however, Claverhouse found himself at odds with the duke of Queensberry, and in 1683 went to join James in Newmarket to seek his support against his Scottish opponents. James backed him, and his backing gave Claverhouse immunity from his political enemies, especially when the duke became king. James VII made Claverhouse a privy counsellor in 1685, a major general in 1686, provost of Dundee in 1688 and, after he had gone to England with Scottish reinforcements for his army at the time of the Dutch invasion, Viscount Dundee. After James's accession, Claverhouse was again put in charge of raiding parties against field conventiclers, presiding over the so-called killing time. In May 1685 he notoriously had one of their leaders, John Brown, shot dead after discovering arms in his house. This summary execution shocked contemporaries and later historians, but does not appear to have affected Claverhouse, for he reported that, 'I caused shoot him dead, which he suffered very inconcernedly'.[9] In his view, the likes of Brown were rebels and traitors who deserved no quarter.

The regime was challenged more seriously that May when the earl of Argyll landed in Scotland and raised a real rebellion. He had refused to take the oaths passed by the Edinburgh parliament in 1681, and had avoided arrest on a charge of treason by fleeing to the Dutch Republic. In his absence he had been attainted. While in the Netherlands he had plotted with other exiles, including Monmouth, to foment an uprising when James succeeded. Monmouth had apparently planned to accompany the earl but had been persuaded instead to raise a separate rebellion in England. Argyll raised between £9,000 and £10,000, most of it from a wealthy widow, Ann Smith. This enabled him to buy three ships and weapons for 8,000 men. He sailed to the Orkneys and then made his way to Argyllshire where he took possession of Dunstaffnage castle, a family seat. He raised his standard in Campbeltown, with the slogan 'No Prelacy,

No Erastianism'. His ships had flown flags with the mottos 'For God, Freedom and Religion' and 'From Popery, heresy and seizure good lord deliver us'.[10] These were scarcely battle cries to rouse the masses, and indeed it is not easy to see what were the positive aims of Argyll's rebellion. His first declaration was mainly directed against the alleged misrule of Charles II, though it declared that James was not a lawful sovereign. It promised to uphold Protestantism, suppress popery and prelacy and to establish a new government, though it did not specify what kind. His second manifesto, 'The Declaration of Archibald Earl of Argyll', denounced James: 'The Duke of York having taken off his mask, and having abandoned and invaded our Religion and Liberties, resolving to enter into the Government and exercise it contrary to law, I think it not only just but my duty to God and my country to use my outmost endeavours to oppose and repress his usurpations and tyranny.' It was clear what Argyll was against, but not what he was for. The Covenanters refused to join him, and he found very little support for his uprising, raising only 2,500 men. By 30 May these had advanced to a location between Dumbarton and Loch Lomond. There they were faced by superior royal troops and retreated to the Clyde. The rebel forces were ruthlessly suppressed, commanders of the government's troops being instructed to 'either kill or apprehend all those who joined with the late Argile against the king'.[11] Argyll tried to escape in disguise but was apprehended and brought to Edinburgh, where he was executed without trial, having been previously attainted. His followers suffered a similar fate or were transported to the West Indies, while his estates in Argyllshire were devastated.

This was a 'fortunate beginning' of James's reign in Scotland, since, as Lord Balcarres later told him, it 'fixed your authority (as unsuccessful rebellions never fail to do)'.[12] One of the ways in which James chose to exploit his authority at this time was by ordering elections to the magistracy of Edinburgh and other towns to be set aside, as he intended to appoint them himself. Another was to insist that Catholics be brought into the administration of his northern kingdom. The earl of Dumbarton was made commander-in-chief of the forces there. Twenty-six Catholics, including the duke of Gordon and the earl of Seaforth, were appointed as commissioners of the excise in their counties notwithstanding their failure to take the test. Thus did the king's promise to the Scottish parliament that he would defend the 'Religion as established by law' seem to wither on the vine.

Just as the suppression of Monmouth's rebellion was followed by a struggle for power in England between Rochester and Sunderland, so that of Argyll's gave rise to a contest among Scottish ministers. James had initially confirmed all his brother's appointments in Scotland 'till he had more tyme to send doune new commissions'.[13] Queensberry had been confirmed as Treasurer and Perth as Chancellor. Queensberry now found himself opposed by Perth and the Secretary, John Drummond, earl of Melfort, who was Perth's brother. There was a closer parallel between the English rivalry of Rochester and Sunderland and the Scottish struggle between Queensberry and the Drummond brothers. Queensberry was a relative of Rochester's while Perth and Melfort were protégés of Sunderland. As in England, too, James showed a preference for the Lord Treasurer, and it took until February 1686 for his rivals to oust him. In December 1685 all three were in London, and the king summoned them to attend him on 3 December, when he urged them to put aside their differences. They agreed to feign friendship in public, even though Perth told James that Queensberry 'was an atheist in religion, a villain in friendship, a knave in business and a traitor in his carriage to him'.[14]

The Drummond brothers eventually outmanoeuvred Queensberry because they favoured the king's Catholicising efforts. Perth even declared to the king his own conversion to Catholicism when he visited London in 1685. He claimed to have been converted after reading papers on religion by Charles II which the king gave him to read. His conversion has ever since been suspected of opportunism, though a case has been made for its sincerity.[15] To give him the benefit of the doubt, it does seem that he genuinely believed that he would not only have to quit office, but even to leave the country if his conversion became public knowledge. When it did, in November, the duke of Hamilton, no friend to Queensberry, observed that even the Treasurer's opponents 'begins now to talke that it's better to bear his houmers than to joine in Councills with a popish Chancellor'.[16] Despite his critics, in December Perth opened a chapel in Edinburgh. This flagrantly violated a Scottish Act of Parliament of 1560 which made attendance at mass criminal, imposing the death penalty for the third offence. Perth reassured James that 'Scotland is not England' and that 'measures need not be too nicely keept with this people, nor are wee to be suffered to imagine that your Majesty is not so far above your laws as that you cannot dispense with them'.[17] Perth's brother also declared his conversion early in 1686. News of their conversions coincided with other revelations of the king's support of Catholicism. James granted pensions of over £12,000 to his co-religionists. As in England, he muzzled the pulpits and the press, forbidding their criticising the Catholic faith. One minister was prohibited from preaching after declaring that he would as soon believe the moon was made of green cheese as in transubstantiation. When James Glen, a bookseller, received the order not to sell any anti-Catholic books, 'he answered the Masters of the Privy Counsell, that he had one book in his chop which condemned Popery very directly, and he desired to know if he might sell it, meaning the Bible'.[18]

Such high-profile moves in favour of Catholics provoked a Protestant reaction. Clergy of the established church had to be rebuked for preaching virulent sermons against 'papists' and 'popery'. One of the most out-spoken, a minister in Selkirk, was deprived of his living. There were anti-Catholic riots in Edinburgh. On 24 January 1686, a crowd of apprentices and women insulted Catholics leaving the house of a priest, calling them papist dogs. Soldiers looked on passively or even encouraged the insults. On 31 January the house itself was attacked, stones being thrown at the windows during a communion service. The countess of Perth was pelted with mud. On this occasion the Lord Provost brought guards to protect the worshippers. Some drunken soldiers shot into the crowd, killing three people. They apprehended a ringleader who was ordered to be flogged through the streets of Edinburgh on 1 February. While the punishment was being carried out, the offender was rescued by the crowd. On hearing rumours of a plan to 'destroy all papists' on 7 February, the authorities took them seriously enough to ensure that no further violence was offered to Catholics.[19] James himself wrote to defend Perth and to demand that the suspects should be tortured to get at the truth.

The disturbances played into the hands of the Drummond brothers in their campaign against Queensberry, since they persuaded James that the duke had lost control of the Scottish capital. In February he was dismissed as Treasurer and as governor of Edinburgh castle. The Treasury was put into commission, while the Catholic duke of Gordon replaced Queens-berry as governor. Of Gordon's appointment James commented, 'I thought that necessary at this tyme to make that towne have more regard for my commands and civiler to the Catholicks, by seeing it in the hands of one of that persuasion'.[20] Although Queensberry was placed on the Treasury commission, not being finally stripped of his posts until June, Perth headed it. He and Melfort also got the king to appoint the duke of

Hamilton as one of the commissioners, and at the same time to grant him a pension. The alliance with Hamilton was a coup for the Drummond brothers, since he carried considerable influence in Protestant circles, being a leading Presbyterian peer. Perth had skilfully exploited a dispute between Hamilton and Queensberry over accommodation in Holyroodhouse. Hamilton claimed the right to dispose of rooms in the palace, and accused Queensberry of occupying more than had been allocated to him. Perth intervened in the dispute on Hamilton's side, and persuaded the king to give directions that only a royal warrant to the duke could give anybody the right to lodgings in Holyrood. Melfort also looked after Hamilton's interests with James, getting the king to appoint Sir George Lockhart as president of the Court of Session, which the duke had solicited. Such cultivation of Hamilton paid dividends when they got him on their side in the struggle for power with Queensberry.

Indeed, Perth and his brother Melfort now became the king's most trusted advisers for Scottish affairs. They assured James that the Edinburgh parliament would acquiesce in his proposal to repeal the penal laws, and replace the test with an oath of allegiance in order for Catholics to be appointed to offices under the Crown. Members of the secret committee of the Privy Council warned that it would not be so easy to persuade the parliament. James reacted with characteristic anger and summoned three members of the committee, one of them the duke of Hamilton, to London. There they insisted that there would be insuperable difficulties in obtaining parliamentary support for his plans unless they included toleration for Protestants as well as Catholics. The duke of Hamilton thought that James had taken the point, for he wrote to his wife that 'the king expresses a great dale of justice and moderation and I hope wee shall all be very happy under his government'.[21] On his return to Scotland, however, he soon found that this was not to be.

In April, the earl of Moray, who had replaced Queensberry as commissioner, and had also announced that he had converted to Catholicism, opened a new session of the Scottish parliament. In the view of one critical observer, Moray demonstrated 'small skill in managing so ticklish an affair, where there required no small art to be used, in a meeting full of bad impressions, difficult humours and interests'.[22] He read a letter from the king urging the members to repeal the penal laws against Catholics, and to confer upon them the 'security under our government which others of our subjects have'.[23] The king clearly wanted them to pass an Act tolerating Catholics. The bishop of Edinburgh preached a sermon at the opening of the session in which he exhorted the members 'to comply in what was desired for the repealing of the laws against Papists, for first it was their duty so to do as being subjects, secondly it was their interest'.[24] An Act was subsequently drawn up by a committee to give them liberty of conscience, though not liberty of worship except in private houses, while retaining the penal laws against them on the statute book. Even this minor concession met with much opposition, particularly from the bishops, when debated in the full parliament. The session was adjourned from 29 April to 6 May while an answer to the King's letter was drafted. When they reconvened they discussed the reply to the king, which contained a clause concerning the request to relax the penal laws against Catholics, stating that 'we shall in obedience to your Majesty's commands, and with tenderness to their persons, take the same into our serious and dutiful consideration, and go as great lengths therein as our consciences will allow, not doubting that your Majesty will be careful to secure the Protestant Religion established by law'.[25] They then adjourned their meeting until 13 May. James felt obliged to prorogue the session on 15 June. He even declined to have the answer to his letter published, though this had been the practice previously. The new Scottish ministry had failed to carry his measures through the Edinburgh parliament which had, up to that point, been much more cooperative than its English counterpart. A scapegoat was found in another manager of the parliament for the court, George Mackenzie, a staunch Stuart supporter whom James had made Viscount Tarbat within days of his accession. Tarbat had assured the king that the Toleration Act was attainable, and even 'shewn him the Rolls of the Members of Parliament, and pricked doune who he thought would be for it, and who against it'.[26] In the event, however, even the Lords of the Articles had not played the compliant role expected of them. They discussed the bill for Catholic relief before presenting it to parliament, when the decision to introduce it was passed by only 18 votes to 14.

The debates in this parliament displayed 'the first symptoms of discontented humour, or jealousy, that appeared in Scotland'.[27] According to the duke of Hamilton, but for his intervention there would have been a motion to have the chancellor turned out because of his religion.[28] The Episcopalians were alarmed not only by the concessions to Catholics, but also by the undermining of the established church, which raised the spectre of a Presbyterian ascendancy. As the earl of Balcarres bluntly told

James later, 'the terror of bringing back a party who had ever lain at catch for the bringing down of the Monarchy, and that had cost your predecessors so much time, blood and treasure to humble, made even your firmest and faithfulest servants comply with your demands but with an unwilling mind'.[29] The king also alienated Episcopalians by depriving the bishop of Dunkeld of his bishopric without assigning any reason, though it was assumed it was for his vigorous anti-Catholic views. As the duke of Hamilton observed, such actions gave people just grounds to say 'that nothing less is intended then the overturning of the protestant religion'.[30]

As in England, James looked to alternative sources of support. Five privy counsellors were struck off, while the earl of Dundonald, a Presbyterian, and the earls of Seaforth and Traquair, both Catholics, were admitted to the Privy Council. James suspended elections in town councils and nominated Catholics and Presbyterians to run them. When he dissolved parliament on 8 October it became clear that these purges were designed for fresh elections to a new parliament. He announced his intention of instituting a Catholic chapel in Holyrood and ordered the judges not to molest Catholics. On 23 November, 'the King's Yaught arrived from London at Leith, with the Popish altar, vestments, images, Priests, and other dependers, for the Popish Chapell in the Abbey'.[31]

On 12 February 1687, James proclaimed an edict of toleration for Scotland, two months before his Declaration of Indulgence in England. It was thought proper to begin there because Scots had acknowledged the king's 'sacred, supreme, sovereign and *absolute power* and authority'.[32] The Proclamation stressed that it was based on 'our sovereign authority, prerogative royal and absolute power, which all our subjects are to obey without reserve'. It allowed 'moderate Presbyterians to meet in their private houses', and 'Quakers to meet and exercise in their Form in any place or places appointed for their worship'. It also did 'suspend, stop and disable all laws, or Acts of Parliament ... against any of our Roman Catholick subjects'.[33] The Proclamation was read in the Privy Council on 17 February and an answer drawn up on 24 February. It acknowledged the king's right to employ whom he pleased in civil or military offices. Some Protestant privy counsellors, however, led by the duke of Hamilton, refused to sign it, for which they were reprimanded. On 10 March the Privy Council received a letter from the king clarifying his intentions regarding moderate Presbyterians, explaining that they were obliged to take the oath of non-resistance spelled out in the edict, swearing to maintain him and his successors 'in the exercise of their ABSOLUTE POWER'. Few Presbyterians were prepared to swear this oath. In April, therefore, he issued a further clarification allowing Presbyterian ministers to preach without taking the oath. Finally, in July he granted unconditional toleration. As Sir John Lauder observed, 'This was great instability of counsell'.[34]

Gilbert Burnet, in exile in the Dutch Republic, published *Some Reflections on His Majesty's Proclamation* in which he claimed 'there is a new Designation of His Majesty's Authority here set forth of his Absolute Power'.[35] Prince William shared his opinion, to James's astonishment and wrath. 'Is it credible that the prince who, according to all appearances, will succeed me can find fault with the words "absolute power"?' he wrote to his ambassador at The Hague. 'For they cannot be taken to mean either the usurping of my subjects' property or constraining anybody in matters of religion. For the first, nobody can accuse me of ever having done it and for the second everyone can see ... that it is not my intention.'[36]

James was so determined to dispense with religious tests for office in Scotland that he sent down an order 'commanding all in office, civil and military, to give up their commissions, and take out new ones without taking the test'.[37] He himself started the ball rolling in June 1687 by issuing a new commission for the Scottish Privy Council, to which the counsellors were admitted without taking the test. Instead of granting dispensations to individuals, as in England, the king instructed Scottish officials to take out remissions against prosecution for breach of the penal laws. To add insult to injury, these were to be bought from the Scottish Secretary Melfort, who charged £7 per remission, together with a fee to his agent in Scotland, James Stewart, who charged a further £1. Stewart, a Presbyterian lawyer who returned from exile in Holland after the Declaration of Indulgence, was 'looked upon as an inveterate enemy to the established government both in Church and State'.[38] A protest from the Privy Council led James to drop the scheme.

Stewart was one of the few 'whig collaborators' in Scotland. Where, in England, James made a genuine attempt to replace the Anglican power base he had inherited from his brother with a new political elite based on an alliance of Catholics and dissenters, in his northern kingdom his discontent with the Episcopalians did not lead to a similar rapprochement with the Presbyterians. While he came to accept that the English nonconformists were not the republicans and rebels he had suspected them of being during the Exclusion crisis, and could be converted into loyal subjects, he was not prepared to make similar allowances with Scottish Protestants other than the Quakers, whom Robert Barclay and William Penn convinced him were pacifists who did not offer a threat to the peace of the kingdom. Only 'moderate' Presbyterians were offered toleration in Scotland, and it was not clear how their moderation was to be gauged.

The result was that toleration was perceived as being on offer mainly to Catholics in the northern kingdom. This perception was reinforced in June 1687 when James revived the Order of the Thistle. It was meant to be the Scottish equivalent of the Order of the Garter, and to be the highest honour to which Scots could aspire. Melfort was convinced that this would be the case, saying that the revival of the Order 'had effects beyond my expectations so that I would not give a farthing betwixt the Garter and it'.[39] Yet the king made it clear that his co-religionists would be specially honoured. He 'chose only those Scottish peers who were Catholics, by conversion or birth, to be his first knights of the Order of the Thistle. Chief among them were the Drummond brothers.'[40]

James nevertheless felt that the moderate Presbyterians and Quakers as well as the Catholics would welcome the Proclamation and support his aim of removing all disabilities from them. He conducted a similar poll of public opinion as the three questions he put to the political nation in England. In Scotland he commissioned Perth, Tarbat and Balcarres 'to inquire at all the Officers of State, the Judges, and the officers of the army, their opinion and consent under their hands for taking off the penal statutes and test'. As Balcarres later told him, 'most of them, though they consented and signed it, yet had such cruel apprehensions of other things further to be pressed upon them, that it kept them in constant concern and uneasiness'.[41] These tests gave rise to rumours in the summer of 1687 that there was to be a new parliament and that Tarbat was to be the commissioner. By the spring of 1688 these rumours intensified, as did discontent with the king. 'Our archbishops does declair they will never be for alloweing a tolleration or takeing away the penall laws or Test', the duke of Hamilton informed his son in March, remarking that everybody expected a parliament to be held soon, although few thought that it would have more success than the last.[42]

'All these discontents were but like smothered fire', Balcarres observed, 'until the birth of the Prince of Wales.'[43] The proclamation that a Catholic son and heir had been born was greeted with as little enthusiasm in Scotland as it had been in England. 'The business of the new Prince is so much suspected in Scotland', a spy reported to William of Orange, 'that when the news of it were, with great solemnity, made known to the people by the Chancellor, as he was attended with very few of the nobility ... so in his acclamations of joy and waving of his hat he was scarce seconded by one of a great multitude of spectators.'[44] There was, however, no concerted action to offset the consequences of the birth, such as the English conspirators engaged in with the invitation to William of Orange. James was still in a stronger position north of the border than he was in the south. It was not until he withdrew troops from Scotland to reinforce his army in England to counter the Dutch invasion that resistance to his rule became manifest. Discontent with the prospect of a Catholic succession was demonstrated towards the end of 1688 in an outbreak of attacks upon chapels and 'mass houses'. There were pope-burning processions in Glasgow and Edinburgh. The Catholic chapel in Holyrood Palace was sacked, as were the residences of prominent Catholics including Perth. Perth fled the capital on 10 December.

It is generally held that the Scots were 'reluctant revolutionaries' who awaited the outcome of events in England before reacting against James. The Revolution was consequently imported into Scotland.[45] Against this it has been vigorously argued that the Revolution had a momentum of its own north of the border.[46] However, where the Anglican clergy, led by the seven bishops, were at the forefront of the resistance to James, their Episcopalian counterparts in Scotland were reticent, despite their objections to his policy of toleration, because they had as much to lose as he did from the collapse of his regime. At the same time there were Scots in William's entourage at The Hague. Prominent among them were Gilbert Burnet, the future bishop of Salisbury, and Robert Ferguson. While these had more of an English than a Scottish agenda, their ranks also included the earl of Argyll, son of the executed rebel, William Carstares, Sir James Dalrymple of Stair and James Johnston, who were concerned to secure Scotland for the Prince of Orange. After William's invasion, a number of Scots in his army, led by the earls of Argyll, Forfar, Leven and Sutherland, offered proposals to him 'whereby his highness's designs may be facilitated and quicklier expeded'.[47]

Ist. That seeing the knowledge of the true case of the Kingdom of Scotland cannot better be attained than by the information of those who are under the government and that ther cannot be a more effectual way

for settling the nation than by inviting the Lords and Barons of the coun-
trey and the ordinare number of deputies from the royal burrows to come
together, your highness will be pleased to invite them to convene at
Edenbrugh the   day of   next to come to deliberate & resolve what
is necessary in this present exigent for settling the nation according to the
ancient constitution thereof & for secureing religion & liberty therein
against popery & arbitrary government & for obtaining the quiet &
content of the people.

This initiative was endorsed by prominent Scots, led by the duke of
Hamilton, who waited upon William when he arrived in London, and
urged him to take upon himself the government of Scotland. Subsequently he convened a Convention which met in Edinburgh in March
1689. It proceeded to make a settlement significantly more radical than
that of the English Convention. Thus it asserted that James had 'forfaulted'
his Scottish throne through having 'invaded the fundamental constitution
of the Kingdom and altered it from a legal limited monarchy to an arbitrary despotic power'. By using the term 'forfault' it ensured that the claim
of his son and heir was also void.[48]

At the same time, by abolishing episcopacy the Convention also
ensured that there would be a formidable body in Scotland which would
remain loyal to both James and his son. Jacobitism was consequently
much more formidable north of the border than in England. Support for
the exiled Stuarts was strongest not among the highland clans of the Great
Glen, as is often assumed, but in the lowland coastal strip between Fife
and Aberdeen, where Episcopalianism was strongly entrenched. Episcopalians regarded the Revolution as a disaster which had robbed them of
their birthright, and they looked to James VII, and after his death to his
son James VIII, to restore it along with the legitimate ruling house.

The Revolution might have been 'bloodless' as far as the English were
concerned, but it was not for the Scots. On the contrary, John Graham,
Viscount Dundee, better remembered by his former title of Claverhouse,
led a secession from the Edinburgh Convention and raised James's standard. He was joined by Scots loyal to the Stuarts, together with an Irish
Gaelic contingent from the Isle of Rathlin, and laid siege to Blair Atholl.
Government forces sent to raise the siege were defeated on 27 July at the
battle of Killiecrankie. Dundee was among those killed in the conflict, and
his followers were routed at Dunkeld the following month. Nevertheless

their cause survived, and Dundee was succeeded as its leader by the earl of Seaforth, until he surrendered to William's troops in October 1690. There were subsequent skirmishes until peace was concluded in June 1691 at Achallader. A technical breach of its terms by the MacDonalds of Glencoe led to their massacre by the Campbells in February 1692, an event that was to live in infamy. Jacobitism remained a major force in Scottish politics not only while James VII was alive but until the defeat of his grandson 'Bonnie' Prince Charlie at Culloden in April 1746.

Notes and references

1 Fountainhall, ii, 815.

2 *Memoirs touching the Revolution in Scotland,* Colin, Earl of Balcarres (Edinburgh, 1841), p. 2.

3 Fountainhall, ii, 624. James dealt with the Privy Council quite arbitrarily, sending them 'hectoring' letters. Ibid., p. 671.

4 Clarke, *Life,* ii, 10. The fact that it was also the day of his coronation in London, and that of St George, the patron saint of England, might have rubbed some of the shine off this gesture to Scottish opinion.

5 HMC 44th report, *Buccleuch and Queensberry MSS*, p. 91.

6 *Acts of the Parliaments of Scotland*, eds T. Thomson and C. Innes (12 vols, Edinburgh, 1814–75), viii, 459; *The Proceedings of the Parliament in Scotland* (Edinburgh, 1685).

7 HMC 44th report, *Buccleuch and Queensberry MSS,* p. 107.

8 Lord Macaulay, *The History of England from the Accession of James II*, ed. Sir Charles Firth (6 vols, Oxford, 1913), i, 492. David Ogg described the legislation passed by James's Scottish parliament as 'the Nuremberg decrees of seventeenth-century Scotland'! *England in the Reigns of James II and William III* (Oxford, 1984), 174.

9 HMC 44th report, *Buccleuch and Queensberry MSS,* p. 292.

10 Richard L. Greaves, *Secrets of the Kingdom: British radicals from the Popish Plot to the Revolution of 1688–1689* (Stanford, 1992), p. 279.

11 Rosalind K. Marshall, *'A calendar of the correspondence in the Hamilton Archives at Lennoxlove'* (PhD thesis, Edinburgh, 1970), appendix, volume 3, p. 591, Committee of Council to Marquis of Atholl, 31 May 1685. Atholl was ordered to execute 100 of 'the chief ringleaders'.

12 Balcarres, p. 2.

13 Fountainhall, ii, 616.

14 *Hamilton Archives*, p. 605. Perth to Hamilton, 3 Dec. 1685.

15 A. Joly, *James Drummond Duc de Perth 1648–1716* (Lille, 1934), pp. 131–64.

16 *Hamilton Archives*, p. 604, Hamilton to his son the earl of Arran, 19 Nov. 1685.

17 Quoted in Tim Harris, 'Reluctant revolutionaries? Scotland and the Revolution of 1688–89', *Politics and the Political Imagination in Later Stuart Britain*, ed. by Howard Nenner (London, 1997), p. 101.

18 Fountainhall, ii, 699, 717. Glen was imprisoned in November 1687 for selling *The Root of Romish Rites, Ceremonies, and Haeresies, proveing Popery to be only Paganisme and Judaisme revived*. Ibid., p. 830.

19 *The Register of the Privy Council of Scotland*, xii, 92–97, 'A true account concerning the late tumult in Edinburgh'.

20 HMC 44th report, *Buccleuch and Queensberry MSS,* p. 153.

21 *Hamilton Archives*, p. 614.

22 Balcarres, p. 3. The crude devices of dismissing judges, removing privy counsellors and cancelling pensions were used as 'warning shots . . . to terrify and divert other Members of Parliament from their opposition'. Fountainhall, ii, 723.

23 *His Majesties most gracious letter to the parliament of Scotland*, quoted in Harris, 'Reluctant revolutionaries?', p. 102.

24 Morrice MSS P, p. 536.

25 Ibid., p. 537.

26 Fountainhall, ii, 736.

27 Balcarres, p. 2.

28 *Hamilton Archives*, p. 616.

29 Balcarres, p. 3.

30 *Hamilton Archives*, p. 618.

31 Fountainhall, ii, 763. The chapel was consecrated on 30 November, St Andrew's Day.

32 Clarke, *Life*, ii, 107.

33 *By the King a Proclamation . . . 12 Feb 1687*.

34 Fountainhall, ii, 792.

35 Bruce Lenman, 'The poverty of political theory in the Scottish Revolution of 1688–1690', *The Revolutions of 1688–9: Changing perspectives*, ed. Lois Schwoerer (Cambridge, 1992), p. 248. Burnet was indicted for treason in Edinburgh on 14 April 1687.

36 John Miller, *James II* (London, 2000), p. 176.

37 Balcarres, p. 3.

38 Ibid., pp. 3–4.

39 *Hamilton Archives*, p. 640.

40 Matthew Glozier, 'The earl of Melfort, the Court Catholic Party and the Foundation of the Order of the Thistle, 1687', *Scottish Historical Review*, vol. lxxix (2000), 233. Glozier argues that the idea for the Order was not the king's but Melfort's, and that James was in effect in the Scottish Secretary's cypher. While he undoubtedly relied heavily on Melfort's advice

regarding the situation in Scotland, as in England James was ultimately his own man. It is a mistake many historians have made to attribute his policies to the influence of particular ministers. At the end of the day James was determined to be king indeed and to make his own decisions.

41 Balcarres, p. 5.

42 *Hamilton Archives*, pp. 641, 660.

43 Balcarres, p. 6.

44 *CSPD 1687–9*, p. 389.

45 Ian Cowan, 'The reluctant revolutionaries: Scotland in 1688', *By Force or by Default? The Revolution of 1688–9,* ed. Eveline Cruickshanks (Edinburgh, 1989), pp. 65–81.

46 Tim Harris, 'Reluctant revolutionaries?'.

47 Nottingham University Library, Portland MSS PWA/2179/19a. The other proposers were the Lords Elphingtons, Cardross, Stairs, Sir Patrick Hume and Sir Duncan Campbell 'who have joined with his highness & are in armes under his command for persueing the ends of his declarations'.

48 Harris, 'Reluctant revolutionaries?', p. 110.

Chapter Six

James and Ireland

In James II's reign, Ireland, as ever, was haunted by its history. It was largely Roman Catholic, but the Catholics themselves were divided between the native Irish and the 'old' English. The natives, mainly Gaelic speaking, had been conquered in the Middle Ages by invaders from England who looked down disdainfully on the 'O's and the Macs who by ten to one exceeded the others in numbers'.[1] But they in their turn had been superseded by Protestants from Britain in the late sixteenth and seventeenth centuries. Vast territories in Ireland had been taken from the native Irish and 'old' English alike, by Protestant Englishmen under Elizabeth, by Scottish Presbyterians under James VI and I, and by Cromwellian adventurers during the Interregnum. The Elizabethan settlements had expanded the area of the Pale round Dublin, for the most part with Anglican members of the Church of Ireland. Trinity College Dublin had been founded to educate students to become clergymen of the established church. The Presbyterians had gone mainly from Scotland to Ulster. An Irish Catholic warned James shortly after his accession: 'from my certain knowledge of that part of the North that lies next Scotland, I meane the Counties of Down and Antrim and the most part of the counties of Derry and Donegal ... there are five disaffected Presbiteriens for one Catholic or Protestant subject and in the sea port towns scarce any inhabitants but Fanatics'.[2] The Cromwellian settlements had virtually completed the conquest of Ireland by the British.

By 1660 the Catholics, who comprised three-quarters of the population, held less than 10 per cent of the land. The situation was complicated at the Restoration not only because most Catholics had been royalists in the civil war, but also because many Protestants, especially the Anglo-Irish adherents of the Anglican Church of Ireland, had supported the king too. In 1662 the Irish parliament passed an Act of Settlement which tried to resolve the problem by confirming the title of those who had acquired land during the Interregnum, while obliging them to relinquish some to compensate the royalists who were Protestant, and even some who were Catholics. This involved quite considerable redistribution, especially since more cases came to light claiming compensation than had been envisaged in 1662, so that in 1665 an Explanatory Act had to be passed making further adjustments in favour of leading royalists of both persuasions. Although this left the Protestants in the ascendancy, and satisfied some prominent Catholic families, it left the bulk of the population resentful of the Protestant Ascendancy and prepared to challenge it when the time came after James became king.

Towards the end of 1684, Charles II had designated the earl of Rochester as Lord Lieutenant of Ireland, but he never crossed the Irish sea and on James's accession became Lord Treasurer. The powerful duke of Ormonde expected to replace him as Lord Lieutenant, but instead James appointed the archbishop of Armagh and the earl of Granard to be Lords Justices. His instructions to them, issued on 27 March 1685, gave little indication of a new approach to Irish concerns. They urged the justices to pay special attention to the established Church of Ireland, and to ensure that suitable ministers were presented to its livings as they became vacant. Later, as we shall see, James was to deliberately leave them vacant in order to appropriate their revenues for Catholic priests. They were also to take particular notice of the revenues 'and increase the profits of the same'.[3] The only hint that James planned any new initiatives in Ireland were that he required them to revive the prerogative Court of Castle Chamber, and to allow Catholics to participate in civil and military affairs. Otherwise the instructions were routine.

While they contained directions for the command of the army, however, these were shortly afterwards put under Richard Talbot, an old comrade in arms of the new king. Talbot was notorious for his heavy drinking, lying and swearing, and a propensity to avenge perceived insults by duelling. In Charles II's reign he had even had the audacity to challenge Ormonde to a duel, an outrage which the king chastised by imprisoning Talbot. His enemies, and they were many, thought his insolence and hot temper bordered on insanity. Yet he clearly impressed James as a man of action with forceful ideas, a soldier like himself who made a refreshing change from the politicians he had to deal with most of the time. Such was the impression Talbot made upon the king that he was elevated to the peerage as earl of Tyrconnel in May, just before he went to Ireland. While

Argyll's and Monmouth's rebellions were in progress, Tyrconnel kept a watch on the Ulster Presbyterians, who were suspected of complicity with the rebels. He used their alleged disloyalty as an excuse to disarm them and to purge any who were suspected of complicity with the rebellion in the army. These included men who had been armed at the time of the Popish Plot in 1678, whom James considered to be disaffected to him.

Over the summer of 1685, Tyrconnel became embroiled in the struggle for power at James's court between the earls of Rochester and Sunderland, siding with the latter. In September 1685 the earl of Clarendon, Rochester's brother, was appointed Lord Lieutenant of Ireland. Tyrconnel regarded this as a threat to his own position. He wrote to James to protest that Clarendon's appointment 'dos soe terreffye your Catholick subjects hear … by lodging your authority in a person from whom they have so little reason to expect any favour'.[4] When Clarendon arrived in Ireland in January 1686 he took himself off to England to undermine the new Lord Lieutenant at court. Thus he exhibited articles of impeachment against the Vice-Treasurer of Ireland, and even raised charges of a criminal nature about Rochester's conduct. Tyrconnel claimed that the vice-treasurership was worth £6,000 a year, and was of too great a concern to be trusted to a Protestant. The present incumbent, one Price, 'was not only a Protestant but a very eager one and a great instrument of Rochester and a hot supporter of those interests diametrically opposed to his Majesty's present measures'.[5] As James's Lord Treasurer, Rochester had a particular interest in Irish revenues, and Clarendon undertook to follow his advice about improving them. Thus he continued investigations into their administration which his brother had initiated before he became Lord Lieutenant. These retrospective enquiries antagonised some of those investigated, such as Sir William Talbot, so that, as Clarendon was informed, 'the height of their impudence is such that they spare not your Lordship'.[6] Reform of the revenue administration also brought about the first overt criticism from Tyrconnel, not because he objected to it, but because he thought he could make a better job of it.

Clarendon was hardly settled in his new post than he began to complain that his authority was being bypassed. On 25 March he wrote to the earl of Sunderland stressing that he was 'Chief Governor', and asking him to 'excuse the moan I make to you in laying before you how little I shall be made in the opinion of people here without some support from your Lordship, when so many and great alterations are made here, and I know nothing of them but from common fame'.[7]

When Tyrconnel returned from a visit to England in the summer of 1686, he had a commission giving him charge of military matters in Ireland. Clarendon, upon hearing that James had given him the commission, was reluctant to believe it, thinking it was 'more for the King's disservice to have it thought he has one here whom he will not trust, than it will be to my disrepute'.[8] 'It is a new method of doing business', he later confided to Rochester, 'that all that the King thinks fit to have done should be performed by those in subordinate authority, and he, who is vested in all the power the King can give him, must sit like an ass and know nothing.'[9] In exasperation, Clarendon complained to Sunderland that he had 'some reason to believe that it is designed to make further changes amongst the officers of the Army here, though it has not been thought fit to acquaint me therewith ... I cannot believe the King will approve of that method of proceeding, which must certainly render his Chief Governor very little in the opinion of those who are to obey him'.[10] Unfortunately for the Lord Lieutenant, James was all too ready to undermine his authority. Tyrconnel proceeded to replace 'English' soldiers with 'Irish natives', many of whom spoke only Gaelic, while Clarendon was instructed to alter the judiciary in favour of Catholics 'of old Irish race'. He wished, if Catholics were to be appointed to Irish offices, they would be sent over from England and not recruited in Ireland. As he ruefully expressed it in a letter to Rochester, 'I believe it was never yet known, that the sword and the administration of justice were put into the hands of a conquered people'.[11] In his view, 'the great contention here was more between English and Irish than between Catholic and Protestant'.[12] 'It is not so much the King's employing Roman Catholics in the army which disquiets men', he observed to the earl of Sunderland, 'as that there are such from whom, by their own words and actions, they fear to be oppressed instead of being protected.'[13] Such fears led to an exodus of many of the 'English' back to England, disrupting the trade of Ireland which Clarendon was concerned to promote.[14]

Clarendon did his best to allay people's fears of the consequences of James II's policies in Ireland. Thus he issued a proclamation granting indemnity for any words spoken against James before he became king. He also urged James to assure his subjects in Ireland by issuing a proclamation that there would be no undoing of the Act of Settlement. Consequently, when Tyrconnel again went to England in August 1686, with a view to persuading James to revise the settlement, the reassurances

Clarendon had given the 'English' that their property was secure were contradicted. Tyrconnel was accompanied to England by Sir Richard Nagle, a Catholic lawyer, who left London before him, and wrote to him from Coventry a letter objecting to the king's confirmation of the Act of Settlement. In it he wrote that 'he that hath a resolution to establish the Catholic religion cannot imagine that the way of doing the same is to confirm the most considerable interest there in the hands of the Protestants and to take away all the hopes of the Catholic proprietors'.[15]

Clarendon was well aware that Tyrconnel, in collusion with the earl of Sunderland, was undermining his position in England, with the queen as well as with the king, and that his tenure of the lord lieutenancy would soon be terminated. His hunch was correct. In October he received a list of five 'heads sent by His Majesty's command to the Lord Lieutenant of Ireland'.[16] These were complaints about Clarendon's behaviour laid before the king by Tyrconnel. The first was that he had confirmed appointments to corporations despite Tyrconnel's objections to them, while the fifth complained that he had not acted on the king's directions to put Catholics on the corporation of Dublin. The second was that he had allowed disbanded soldiers to keep their arms when 'to leave men that must be displeased for being disbanded with arms in their hands' was 'against all prudence and reason'.[17] The third was that he had recalled an officer from raising men for a regiment of guards, thus countermanding Tyrconnel's orders. The fourth claimed that, although he had consented to the changes in favour of Catholics, he showed that he did not approve of them. As Clarendon riposted, 'what account can a man give of his looks?'[18] Although he defended himself against all the charges, and wrote a grovelling letter to the king, he knew that his days as Lord Lieutenant were numbered. This became clearer when he received a letter from Rochester conveying 'the terrible news of the king's displeasure', who thought his reply unconvincing.[19]

The decline in Rochester's influence with the king was rapidly diminishing the credit of the Hyde brothers at court. For Clarendon, although the elder, was very much the junior partner, as he readily acknowledged. He accepted that his tenure of office could not long outlast that of Rochester. On 8 January 1687 he learned that his brother had resigned, that he had been recalled to England and that Tyrconnel was to be appointed Lord Deputy for the government of Ireland. Although the tetchy Tyrconnel took his appointment to the lesser title as a slight, it probably signified no more than that the king had let it be known he would not promote a native Irishman to the post of Lord Lieutenant. James himself supported 'the rough part he was to act, which was reforming the army, calling in the old charters, and setting the corporations so, as he might be sure of having a good Parliament, which he was persuaded no English peer could effect'.[20]

Tyrconnel's ascendancy marked a transition in Ireland from a regime which had fought a rearguard action against the promotion of Catholics to one which actively pursued it. Thus at the end of 1686 Sir Richard Nagle became attorney general of Ireland, while in January 1687 Sir Alexander Fitton replaced Sir Charles Porter as Irish Lord Chancellor. Porter had been universally liked despite his reputation as a rake. Fitton, on the other hand, had been jailed for his implication in a forgery, and was actually released from prison to take up the Lord Chancellorship. The reason became clear when he had his salary raised in April from £1,000 to £1,500 following the announcement of his conversion to Catholicism. Catholic infiltration of the judiciary had begun in 1686 when one had been installed as a justice in each of the Courts of King's Bench, Common Pleas and Exchequer. This progressed to control by the end of 1687, when two of the three justices in each court were Catholics. In November, the Catholic archbishop of Cashel wrote to the Vatican that Tyrconnel 'has now made the army nearly all Catholics, as well commanders and officers as ordinary soldiers. The royal council in Dublin is for the greater part Catholic. The civil officials, both judges and magistrates, are for a greater part Catholic.'[21]

Catholicism was ascendant in the church as well as in the state. Although the Church of Ireland was not directly undermined, as livings became vacant they were left unfilled and their revenues given to Catholic priests. When the dean of Derry announced his conversion to Catholicism he was allowed to retain his deanery. Catholic chapels were established in Dublin castle and the Royal Hospital, while Kilmainham was reconsecrated for Catholic use. The transformation in the government of Ireland was so sudden and extensive that it alarmed many observers. Even James urged caution in the removal of Protestants, saying that nobody should be removed merely on account of their religion. But Tyrconnel took little notice of warnings that he was going too far and too fast, acting so arbitrarily that his Protestant critics called him 'Turk-conel'.[22]

Tyrconnel was aware that if James died without a Catholic heir the outlook for his co-religionists in Ireland was bleak. As an anonymous correspondent informed James in August 1686, Tyrconnel himself had made 'so many enemies that he has reason to pray as it is sayd he often does that he may either dye a month before or at least not outlive your Majestie a month, for if that poor nation be not made considerable during your reign his Lop must not hope for the favour my Lord Strafford had of being legally murther'd by a formal tryal but may wel expect all formality layd aside to be sacrificed to the unbridled fury of the lawless rabble and dissected into little morsels'.[23] The Lord Deputy in fact relied on more than prayer to protect him and his accomplices in the event of James leaving the throne to his Protestant daughter Mary and her Dutch husband. He told his secretary Thomas Sheridan in 1686, 'the Irish would be fools or madmen if, after his death, they should submit to be governed by the Prince of Orange or Hyde's daughter or be longer slaves to England, but rather set up a King of their own, and put themselves under the protection of France'.[24] James responded to Tyrconnel's daring propositions ambivalently. They appealed to his heart but not to his head. The prospect of making at least one of his three kingdoms a safe haven for his fellow Catholics was attractive to him emotionally. At the same time, political calculations urged caution. The Protestants, although in the minority, were too important in Ireland's economy and politics to be completely set aside. To alienate Irish Protestants would also adversely affect his attempts to woo English dissenters. Above all, his commitment to the hereditary principle made him hesitate to break it in the case of Ireland, even if its independence might seem the best solution for the Irish Catholics. Tyrconnel's schemes therefore made very little progress before they were rendered nugatory by the birth of a son to the king and queen in June 1688.

That event, however, precipitated the invasion of England by William of Orange. James appealed to Tyrconnel to send as many troops from Ireland as he could spare, and some four or five thousand, half the forces at the disposal of the Lord Deputy, were sent over. These Irish reinforcements increased fears of the king's intentions towards his English Protestant subjects. Paranoia about these 'Papist teagues' inspired the doggerel song 'Lilliburlero', written by the whig Thomas, earl of Wharton, who later boasted that it had 'whistled a king out of three kingdoms'. It was largely aimed at Tyrconnel, the 'good Talbot ... made a Lord, who with brave lads was coming abroad'. The popularity of the song was astounding. Bishop Burnet claimed that 'the whole army, and at last all people both in city and country, were singing it perpetually'.[25] This testifies to the fear and hatred which Tyrconnel and his Catholic supporters aroused in England. It helps to explain the otherwise inexplicable panic which broke out when James instructed the earl of Feversham to disband his army, and wild rumours escalated that the demobilised Irish soldiers were on the rampage, raping and looting. Although there was no truth in these tales, they nevertheless spread from the south to the north of the country like wildfire. The party sent down from London to rescue James from his captors in Faversham in mid-December encountered checkpoints set up by people to intercept the rampaging Irishmen.

Before James escaped to France, Tyrconnel had tried to persuade him to take a stand in Ireland. James preferred to seek the protection of Louis XIV rather than the Irish Lord Deputy. The French king greeted him emotionally and offered him and his exiled court accommodation at Saint-Germain en Laye. The palace there, a former hunting lodge, suited the exiled monarch perfectly. He could hunt and pray to his heart's content. It seems that, left to his own devices, he was quite prepared to pursue these activities indefinitely. Louis, however, had more important plans for him. He intended to use James to create a diversion from the continental war he was engaged in, by sending him to retrieve his throne through an invasion of Ireland. The French king's ministers, however, were divided on the desirability of this strategy. Seignelay, the minister of marine, was all in favour, whereas Louvois, the war minister, was not. Vauban, the chief military engineer, told Louvois that it was worth a try. 'His last stake is Ireland,' he said of James. 'It appears to me that he ought to go there, where with the help that the King may give him he can get on his legs again and be supported by those of his subjects who remain loyal to him.'[26] Tyrconnel also pleaded with James to go there. 'I beg of you to consider whether you can with honour continue where you are', he wrote on 29 January, 'when you possess a kingdom of your own plentiful of all things for human life.'[27]

The upshot was that James was urged by the French to go to Ireland but that the help they gave him was limited. Although French officers accompanied him, led by Conrad von Rosen, no troops were sent at the time. It is clear from the instructions given to one of the French officers, Maumont, that they were under the command of the French and not the English king. They were ordered to return to France if they judged that

Ireland favoured William of Orange. Otherwise they could assure Tyrconnel that, if he could hold Ireland for James until the following winter, French troops would be sent to reinforce his army not only to resist William, but also possibly to go over to Scotland or England in support of James's claim to their thrones.

James consequently left St Germain on 15 February and went to Brest. While he was there it was noticed that he ate well, which is not surprising considering that he had fasted for twenty-four hours prior to his departure. The following day he rose at five o'clock to attend Mass and left at six. The French ambassador extraordinary sent by Louis XIV to Ireland, the comte d'Avaux, was shocked by the complete lack of secrecy about the expedition, with James indiscreetly revealing his intentions to all and sundry.

James landed in Kinsale on 12 March 1689. Tyrconnel joined him at Cork on 14 March. James paid the Lord Deputy the unusual favour for a king of meeting him at the door of his chamber and embracing him with open arms. He made him a duke and invited him to sit on his right at his table with the duke of Berwick on his left.[28]

The aims of the two men, however, were rather different, and this initial disagreement about the object of the exercise led to its collapse. Tyrconnel wanted James to complete the hegemony of the Catholics which he had instigated. This meant the reversal of the Protestant ascendancy in Ireland. It would also have meant that James could only retrieve his Irish kingdom, for such a policy would have forfeited any hope of regaining the thrones of England and Scotland. Since such hope was forlorn, Tyrconnel was being the more realistic of the two. While in France, James seems to have conceived of the conquest of Ireland as a kind of Catholic crusade, and approached the papacy for help to unite the Catholic powers of Europe against the usurper William. But this project was doomed from the start, for the Pope refused to give James any support, while the Holy Roman Empire stayed as a linchpin of the League against Louis XIV. After his arrival in Ireland, James determined to regain all three of his realms. He gave as his immediate reason for the expedition the defence of Ireland against the forces of William of Orange. But once he had done this he planned to go to England via Scotland, where he expected 25,000 men to join him.[29] The earl of Melfort encouraged the king's ambition to regain all three of his crowns, while the comte d'Avaux sided with Tyrconnel. When James announced an immediate design to go to Scotland, d'Avaux urged him to subdue Ireland first.[30]

The despatches of d'Avaux, indeed, provide not only the fullest account of the Irish expedition but also a caustic commentary on the king's activities there.[31] The ambassador painted a grim picture of complete chaos and incompetence. Immediately after they landed in Kinsale he informed the French king that James often changed his advice and did not always determine in favour of the best. He devoted himself to details and passed lightly over essential concerns. Tyrconnel had raised the impressive number of 45,000 troops, but they were untrained, unarmed except with spikes mounted on sticks, and almost completely unequipped. Raising the resources to bring this army up to scratch was a formidable problem. James tried to solve it by issuing a proclamation 'revaluing a whole range of foreign and English coins', effectively devaluing them by about 5 per cent.[32] He then issued copper and brass coins ultimately to the face value of £1.5 million. This 'gunmoney', as it was later called, in the short run provided funds to equip his forces, which were reduced to a more manageable 35,000. After their defeat, the money became completely worthless.

When James arrived in Dublin on 24 March he set up a secret council consisting of Melfort, Tyrconnel and d'Avaux. James showed his preference for the advice of the Scottish earl over that of the other two. Thus Melfort approved of his going to the siege of Londonderry when Tyrconnel and d'Avaux urged him to stay in Dublin and prepare for a meeting of the Irish parliament. Writs had been issued for a general election the day after James reached Dublin, and the Houses were to meet on 7 May. Draft bills were discussed in the secret committee, but more thorough preparations for the opening might have averted some of the problems that arose during the session. Parliament had not met in Ireland since 1667. Charles II had declined to summon one for the last 18 years of his life. During his own brief tenure of the English throne, James had contemplated calling one, but had thought better of it. The previous Irish parliament had been composed entirely of Protestants. In this one, thanks to the remodelling of corporations by Tyrconnel, the vast majority of the 230 members of the House of Commons who were returned were Catholics, only five or six being Protestants. About two-thirds were 'old English', the remaining one-third representing the 'O's and the Macs'. These raw, inexperienced MPs would need careful management if difficulties were to be avoided. These were predictable given that James summoned the Anglican bishops of the Church of Ireland to the House of Lords. This was a recipe for trouble which required a careful strategy if the king were to get his way. Yet James spent two days at the siege of Londonderry in the forlorn hope that his mere appearance there would shame his subjects into surrender. Instead he was fired upon by the defiant defenders and was forced to withdraw, with considerable loss of face.

Despite this setback he still felt optimistic when he addressed the Irish parliament at its opening in Dublin on 7 May, the only time an English king ever appeared before that body. The French naval victory over the English at Bantry Bay a week before had boosted the morale of his supporters on both sides of the Irish sea. James thanked the members of the Dublin parliament for their support of Tyrconnel, which had put Ireland at his disposal and led him to resolve to go there to expose his own life along with theirs in defence of their liberty and his rights. He was ready to give his assent to all good and salutary laws for the welfare of the nation in general and the growth of trade. He was even prepared to pass a law to relieve those who had suffered from the Act of Settlement as far as it was consistent with reason, justice and the public interest. This clearly fell short of a complete repeal.

The session began by passing laws to James's liking. One Act acknowledged him as the rightful sovereign and condemned the Revolution in England as a usurpation. Another declared that the English parliament could not legislate for Ireland. A move to repeal Poynings' Law, however, which required all legislation passed by the Irish parliament to be approved by the English Privy Council, James disapproved on the grounds that it diminished his prerogative. The Commons responded generously to his request for a revenue of £15,000 a month for thirteen months, raising it to £20,000. The debates on the ways and means of raising it, however, became protracted as the members determined on repealing the Act of Settlement despite the king's resistance to such a measure, and held up supply until he assented to it.

The Catholic majority showed itself in favour of Tyrconnel's schemes when, on 22 June, they repealed the Act of Settlement of 1662, which had left Irish Catholics with less than a quarter of the land in Ireland. James himself had never supported total repeal of the Act. The most he had been prepared to concede was made known when he met Tyrconnel in Chester in August 1687. There he had allowed the Lord Deputy to draw up draft legislation to revise the settlement to give Catholics an equal share with Protestants. The Dublin parliament sought to reverse the settlement completely. James was affronted at this insistence on total repeal, and displayed anger when the members insisted upon it even if it harmed the interests of some Catholics. His outburst of temper, in which ominously his nose bled, showed that he had not learned from his experience with his English parliament how to manage elected assemblies. It only served to make the members more intransigent. They refused to pass any bill until the Act of Settlement was repealed, and for good measure they passed an Act of Attainder against over 2,000 Protestants. These were divided into three categories. The first, a majority, named those who had supported William of Orange. They were declared to be traitors unless they surrendered to James by 10 August and were acquitted in a subsequent trial. The second category listed those who had left Ireland since the arrival of William in England. Unless they returned by 1 September their departure would be regarded as treasonable. The last and smallest category was of those who had crossed the Irish Sea before the Dutch invasion. They were given until 1 October to return, unless James had himself crossed the sea by then – as J. G. Simms commented, 'an optimistic touch' – in which case he would pardon those who gave satisfactory reasons for having left Ireland.[33] Such vindictiveness stood in sharp contrast to the Toleration Act passed at the same time in which the parliament paid lip service to the king's aims, outlined in his speech to the legislature at its opening, that he was always in favour of liberty of conscience.

In truth, James had made a mistake in agreeing to summon the parliament, for it brought out the sharp difference between his objectives and those of the majority of his Irish subjects. He was anxious not to alienate his Protestant subjects in England, whose support was essential if he were to regain his English throne. The members of the Dublin parliament wished to protect the interests of Irish Catholics. Not only did this involve the repeal of the Act of Settlement and the Act of Attainder, it also led to the passing of an Act allowing Catholics to pay tithes to their own priests instead of to the clergy of the Church of Ireland. If this measure had ever been implemented it would have dealt a deadly blow to the established church. James's English aspirations were incompatible with the concerns of his Irish subjects. Even d'Avaux commented on the priority the king gave to England, when he refused to pass a bill which would have allowed raw wool to be exported from Ireland to France. The French ambassador observed, 'he has a heart too English to take any step that could vex the English, and that holds up the woollen business'.[34]

The proceedings of the Irish parliament not only rendered any attempt to regain his other kingdoms completely hopeless, but also made certain that the Protestants in Ulster would support a determined effort by William to conquer Ireland. Their bases at Enniskillen and Londonderry held out despite James's attempts to take them. D'Avaux was convinced that the king's leniency to his Protestant subjects had spoiled any chance of subduing the rebels. The French ambassador saw the war as an Irish conflict between Catholics and Protestants, as did Tyrconnel who insisted that in the whole of Ireland there were at most one hundred Protestants who supported James. 'What is necessary', agreed Louvois, 'is that he should forget that he has ever been King of England and Scotland and think only of what will benefit Ireland and will provide him with means to maintain himself there.'[35] The king, however, regarded the struggle as a civil war in all three of his kingdoms between Jacobites and Williamites. He would not cut the throats of his Protestant subjects in Ireland since this would alienate their co-religionists in England and Scotland. Consequently, when the French commander Conrad von Rosen issued a draconian edict to the men of Londonderry to capitulate, or no quarter would be given when starvation forced them to submit, James was horrified. Melfort claimed that, had Rosen been an Englishman, he would have been hanged. The French ambassador defended the commander's action. He felt that James's attitude was influenced so much by his determination to use Ireland as a mere stepping-stone to England that he had alienated his Irish subjects. If so, he had got the worst of all possible worlds, for he lost Ireland and never stood a chance of regaining his English crown.

The siege of Londonderry lasted from 18 April until relieved from England on 28 July. The day before, the death of Viscount Dundee at the battle of Killiecrankie effectively ended any hope of James's linking up with Jacobites in Scotland. James's plan to use Ireland as a base to invade Scotland was finally scuppered when the duke of Schomberg landed at the head of an army at Bangor in Ulster on 13 August. The king recognised this when he dispensed with Melfort's services in September, and the earl returned to France.

Schomberg's arrival did not mean that James's prospects in Ireland itself were doomed. His opponent was an octogenarian who moved cautiously, determined not to risk his raw recruits in battle. James, who was 57, is sometimes described as being prematurely aged himself. Certainly he was not the military man he had been when he served under Turenne.

D'Avaux was convinced that James was contemplating leaving Ireland after the relief of Londonderry. Although James angrily denied this when Tyrconnel also raised the matter, the French ambassador concluded that he had determined not to leave the country as he had done England without fighting a battle, but would leave after the first defeat. Yet d'Avaux himself left Ireland before the end of 1689. He had lost the confidence not only of James but also of the comte de Lauzun, who replaced Rosen as French commander in November. The ambassador left for France on the same ship that brought Lauzun to Ireland. James was delighted to greet the new commander, who had been responsible for conveying his queen and infant son to France. His arrival also showed that Louis XIV had not despaired of James, despite d'Avaux's caustic despatches. On the contrary, he assured James that reinforcements would be sent to his army.

When the two armies dug in for the winter, therefore, it was by no means certain that the troops sent from England would prevail. Although Schomberg had resisted James's attempts to bring him to battle, he had been obliged to withdraw from Dundalk due to sickness raging through the ranks of his troops. James had at his disposal some 35,000 men. In spring 1689, the 5,000–6,000 reinforcement promised by Louis XIV arrived. The arms supplied by Louis XIV ensured that the deficiencies in James's army which had been noticeable when he first arrived in Ireland had been largely removed. Even d'Avaux grudgingly conceded that its morale was high after the departure of Melfort. William III himself was aware that Schomberg's position was not strong, and reluctantly replaced the aged general in person, arriving at Carrickfergus in mid-June.

The comte de Lauzun had quickly found that d'Avaux's estimates of the unpreparedness of James's army for combat with William had not been exaggerated. He became so convinced that they would be defeated that he advised James to retreat to the River Shannon. James ignored this advice and advanced to meet William at the River Boyne. The battle fought there on 1 July proved decisive. William won a complete victory. James fled back to France as quickly as he could, never to set foot in any of his kingdoms again.

D'Avaux's hunch that James would fight one battle and then quit Ireland proved correct. The French ambassador's caustic view of the king will always colour our assessment of his ultimate failure to keep his Irish kingdom. His account of the king's indecisiveness, inability to see the wood for the trees, and refusal to face facts indicates that James was losing his mental powers. At the same time his admission that James showed the energy of a 20 year old does not suggest that he was ageing physically. The whole Irish episode, rather like the closing months of his reign in England, has a bizarre, almost surreal feel to it. It is sometimes hard to credit that what happened really could have taken place. At the heart of it must be the king's psychological state, to use a modern phrase. James himself might have referred to the state of his soul, for there seems little doubt that, from the turning of the 'Protestant wind' which blew William of Orange down the English Channel in 1688 to the end of his life, James felt that he had been weighed in the balance and found wanting. Providence determined that he would forfeit his crown because he did not deserve to keep it. His heart was not in the expedition to Ireland; he was simply going through the motions. The rest of his life was to be a penance for the sins which had lost him three kingdoms.

Notes and references

1 HMC *Stuart Papers*, pp. vi, 6.

2 William Frazer, 'A series of eight anonymous and confidential letters to James II about the state of Ireland', *Notes and Queries* (1882), 6th series, v, 322.

3 *CSPD 1685*, p. 110.

4 BL Add. MSS 32095, fo. 224, Tyrconnel to James II, Dublin, 29 August 1685.

5 *CSPD 1686*, p. 151.

6 Bodleian Library, Clarendon State Papers, vol. 88, p. 200.

7 *CSPD 1686*, p. 83.

8 Singer, i, 288.

9 Singer, ii, 10.

10 *CSPD 1686,* p. 254.

11 Singer, i, 357.

12 Ibid., i, 296.

13 Ibid., i, 486.

14 How many Protestants left Ireland under James II is disputed. It has been claimed that most, like their counterparts in England, gave the king the benefit of the doubt until the Irish parliament of 1689 threatened the land settlement, and that before then at most 5 per cent crossed the Irish Sea. R. Gillespie, 'The Irish Protestants and James II', *Irish Historical Studies,* xxviii (1992), 124–37.

15 J. G. Simms, *Jacobite Ireland 1685–91* (Dublin, 1969), p. 31.

16 Bodleian Library, Clarendon State Papers, vol. 88, p. 296.

17 Singer, ii, 17.

18 Ibid., ii, 19.

19 Ibid., ii, 39.

20 HMC *Stuart Papers*, vi, 14.

21 Quoted in James McGuire, 'James II and Ireland 1685–90', *Kings in Conflict: The Revolutionary War in Ireland and its aftermath 1680–1750,* ed. W. A. McGuire (Belfast, 1990), p. 53.

22 *Notes and Queries* (1882), 6th series, vi, 3.

23 Ibid.

24 HMC *Stuart Papers*, vi, 8–9.

25 Burnet, *History*, iii, 336.

26 Quoted in F. C. Turner, *James II* (London, 1948), p. 463.

27 Marquise Campana de Cavelli, *Les Derniers Stuarts a Saint-Germain-en-Laye* (2 vols, Paris, 1891), ii, 531. Tyrconnel predicted that James would be in control of Ireland within one month!

28 Ibid., p. 575.

29 Ibid., pp. 509–10, 524–5.

30 *Négociations de M. le comte d'Avaux en Irlande 1689–90*, ed. J. Hogan (Dublin, 1934), p. 49.

31 Pierre Joannon, 'Jacques II et l'expedition d'Irlande après les dépêches du comte d'Avaux', *L'autre exil: Les Jacobites en France au debut du XVIIIe siecle* (1993).

32 Robert Heslip, 'Brass money', *Kings in Conflict: The Revolutionary War in Ireland and its aftermath 1680–1750,* ed. W. A. McGuire (Belfast, 1990), p. 126.

33 J. G. Simms, 'The Jacobite Parliament of 1689', *War and Politics in Ireland 1649–1730*, eds D. W. Hayton and Gerard O'Brien (Belfast, 1986), p. 75.

34 Quoted in Simms, 'The Jacobite Parliament of 1689', p. 79.

35 Turner, *James II*, p. 473.

Chapter Seven

James and North America

James was not only king of England, Scotland and Ireland but also ruled over a number of colonies in the West Indies and along the Atlantic seaboard of North America. When James succeeded his brother to the throne, the West Indian possessions, which included the sugar islands of Barbados and Jamaica, were directly under the Crown, as were New Hampshire, New York and Virginia on the mainland. Although they had elected assemblies, the governors were appointed by the king, and they in turn nominated a council. But other settlements had different polities, and are usually distinguished as charter and proprietary colonies. Connecticut, Massachusetts and Rhode Island in New England had charters which allowed them to be virtually self-governing. Not only were their assemblies elected but so were their councils and governors. In Massachusetts the right to vote for the lower house of assembly, or General Court, was confined to members of the Independent or Congregational Church. They called themselves 'visible saints' and were called Puritans by others. Although the franchise was not confined to church members in Connecticut, nevertheless its assemblies, councils and governors, as in Massachusetts, were generally chosen to uphold a puritan way of life. Rhode Island, by contrast, was known for its practice of religious toleration. Quakers, who were banned in Massachusetts, along with Baptists and other Protestant sects, thrived there. Maryland, New Jersey, North and South Carolina and Pennsylvania were governed by proprietors who had been vested with them by the Stuarts. Thus the first of these proprietary grants, Maryland, had been made to the Catholic Lord Baltimore by Charles I, while the latest, Pennsylvania, was granted to the Quaker William Penn by Charles II in 1681. These proprietors were virtual rulers of their colonies provided they abided by the terms of the royal charters which conferred them. For instance, laws passed by their assemblies had to be confirmed by the Privy Council.

As duke of York, James had been closely involved with the American colonies. In April 1663 a commission to investigate New England was set up under his auspices and staffed by his henchmen Sir William Coventry, John, Lord Berkeley and Sir George Carteret. They drew up a proposal which was put to the Council for Foreign Plantations the following January. It recommended the grant to James of a vast proprietorship in North America, which stretched from Maine to the Delaware Bay, and included the whole of the Dutch colony of New Netherland. When Charles granted this to his brother in March 1664, an expedition was sent out to New Netherland led by Richard Nicholls. Nicholls arrived in the Hudson river and demanded that the Dutch governor, Stuyvesant, surrender to him. While the governor was prepared to resist, the inhabitants urged him to obey Nicholls' demands. Following the surrender of the Dutch colony to Nicholls, it was named after the duke as New York. Its principal towns, New Amsterdam and Orange, were also given the names of his duchies, becoming New York City and Albany. Long Island even became known as Yorkshire, and was divided into three Ridings. James became proprietor not only of New York but also of adjacent New Jersey, or Albania as it was initially called, again after his ducal titles. He ceded the territories of East and West Jersey to his old comrades Lord Berkeley and Sir George Carteret, but kept the government or dominion for himself. Later, when he tried to grant the right of ruling to the proprietors, Charles II objected that it was his and not the duke's to concede. A judicial decision in 1680 appeared to confer the right on James, but it remained in doubt throughout the 1680s. Similar dubiety arose over his concession of the territories on the west bank of the River Delaware to William Penn when Charles II granted him the proprietorship of Pennsylvania in 1681. The three lower counties which James added to the royal grant in 1682, and which ultimately became the state of Delaware, gave rise to much dispute as to whether the right of government had been conceded to Penn along with the proprietorship of the soil. James only reluctantly yielded the lower counties, under pressure from his brother. After he became king, James even issued a *quo warranto* against Pennsylvania, and Penn had his work cut out to get it recalled.

James ruled his own proprietorship of New York with the absolute authority with which he was invested by his brother's charter of 1664. This was reissued in 1674 after the colony's reconquest by the Dutch in the third Anglo-Dutch war, when New York again became New

Amsterdam for over a year. The Dutch finally ceded the colony to the English Crown at the Treaty of Westminster in 1674. Richard Nicholls served as James's deputy governor after his initial conquest of the colony for the duke. He inaugurated what became known as the Duke's Laws. There was no provision for a representative assembly, or for town meetings. As Nicholls observed in a letter to Clarendon in July 1665: 'our new Lawes are not contrived soe Democratically as the rest'.[1] There was even a garrison in New York City, the first regular force in British America. After the final cession of the colony by the Dutch, James sent out as his deputy Sir Edmund Andros, an army officer who had seen service in the West Indies. He was instructed to re-establish the proprietorship and to reinstate the Duke's Laws, which he did with relish as a man of arbitrary disposition. This provoked demands from some settlers for an assembly. When Andros reported this to James, James replied that to yield to them would be 'of dangerous consequence, nothing being more knowne than the aptness of such bodyes to assume to themselves many priviledges wch prove destructive to, or very oft disturbe, the peace of the governmt wherein they are allowed'.[2] The arbitrariness of James's government of his proprietary colony prompted William Penn to observe that 'all men take as the just moddell of government in New York to be the schem & draught in little of his administration of old England at large if the Crown should ever devolve upon his head'.[3]

James, however, was aware of his deputy's difficulties in raising taxes without the consent of the colonists. Indeed, not enough was being raised to recoup his own expenses incurred in setting up his proprietorship, including £2,000 spent on regaining it in 1674. James was anxious to realise a profit from the colony to offset his own financial difficulties. He did, therefore, allow Andros to make out a case for conceding an assembly, which the governor did when he went to England in 1681. The duke's secretary, Sir John Werden, wrote to Andros's deputy 'that we believe his Rll Hs will condescend to the desires of that Colony in granting them equall priviledges in choosing an Assembly ... as the other English plantations in America have'.[4] When Colonel Thomas Dongan was sent to New York to replace Andros, his instructions contained a requirement to convene an assembly there. One duly assembled in October 1683 and sat for three weeks. A second session was held the following year. In 1685, news arrived that James had become king, and the status of New York had changed from a proprietary to a Crown colony. Dongan dissolved the assembly, held new elections, and convened another in October 1685. When the session ended, another was announced for September 1686, but was prorogued before it was held, and the assembly was dissolved in January 1687.

Although it never met again during James's reign, it is clear that the king was not utterly opposed to a representative body in the colony of New York. On the contrary, he was persuaded that one was needed there in order to compete commercially with adjacent colonies. Pennsylvania in particular, which had an assembly from the start, soon moved ahead of New York economically. Philadelphia rapidly outgrew New York City to become the biggest town on the eastern seaboard and its most thriving port.

From the start, James was as much involved with the commerce as with the colonies of North America. He became governor of the Company of Royal Adventurers trading to Africa, incorporated in 1672 as the Royal African Company, which supplied slaves to the American colonies. He was also governor of the Hudson's Bay Company from 1683 until he became king, when he was succeeded by John Churchill. This was not merely an honorary post, for the company became embroiled with French claims to its jurisdiction which had to be resolved in London. The company claimed that its interest in the Bay area was not disputed by France until 1682. In that year, however, French traders seized assets of the company, including a ship manned by English sailors, who were sent as slaves to Martinique. The company protested in the strongest terms to the king.

The adversary stance adopted by New France to English interests in North America led James to adopt a defensive posture there against the French, notwithstanding the cordial relationship he enjoyed with Louis XIV in European concerns. In 1686 the Compagnie du Nord launched an attack led by Pierre Le Moyne d'Iberville on the Hudson's Bay Company's forts around James Bay. The disputes between the two companies were so serious that Louis XIV sent a special envoy, Bonrepos, to England to help his ambassador, Barillon, to resolve them. A draft treaty of neutrality was drawn up in November, but it was not until 1687 that a definitive document could be signed by the two sides. James appointed Sunderland, Middleton and Godolphin as commissioners to negotiate with Bonrepos and Barillon.

It is significant that the king fielded such a heavyweight team to negotiate with the astute and experienced agents of Louis XIV, and that no

Catholic was entrusted with the negotiations. They insisted that the English had the rightful claim to the Hudson's Bay territories in which the company operated and on which, since its launch in 1670, it had invested £200,000. The French replied that they had an equal right, having been involved in the exploration of the area as much as the English since the early seventeenth century. This argument was dismissed as specious, since on that basis the French could also challenge English rights to Pennsylvania and the Carolinas, 'and his Majesty is too much concerned in the consequence of such a position to esteem it of the least validity, since ... his Majesty's plantations aforementioned and other provinces and countrys in America would be laid open to the pretentions and like invasions of the French founded upon so remarkable a precedent as this would be'.[5] What mattered was effective settlement and occupation, which the English had established prior to any French claim to the territory. French settlement in Canada could not be cited as a valid claim to Hudson's Bay since the two areas were distinct,

> and it is to be hoped that it will not now be reputed a dependencie of Canada which would be a pretention not to be advanced between two Crownes that entertain so good a correspondence together; and which would quite destroy the end of the late Treaty of neutrality, since instead of preserving peace in time of warr it will be lookt upon as the occasion of warr in time of peace if soe notorious an invasion should remain unpunisht or satisfaction refused for the losses that have been sustained.[6]

James is often described as an ally of Louis XIV, while England is similarly dismissed as a satellite of France during his reign. In fact James was never formally allied with the king of France, and as these strong words used in the tough negotiations over their respective American territories demonstrate, he was quite prepared to stand up to Louis when he felt that English interests were threatened by the French. In the event, hostilities were averted when a treaty, or 'Instrument for the quieting of all disputes between the English and French in America', was agreed between the two sets of commissioners in November 1687. This established 'that it shall not be lawful for any Governor or commander in chief of the colonies, islands, lands and territories, belonging to either King's Dominions being in America to commit any act of Hostility against or to invade the subjects of the other king'.[7]

The commissioners also discussed disputes arising from French aggression against Indian allies of the English colonists in North America. In 1677, a so-called Covenant Chain had been negotiated at Albany between colonial representatives led by New York and the Iroquois nation. It was in essence a treaty of mutual defence against the French. In 1687 the Governor of Quebec, the marquis de Denonville, launched a massive attack upon some of the Indians who were party to the treaty, destroying their villages, corn and livestock. Dongan reinforced Albany to deter further French attacks but this did not placate the Iroquois. The French complained to the English about the latter's arming of the Indians. When the commissioners addressed the situation they urged the king to 'give them all necessary aid and assistance to oppose the French in case of another invasion'.[8]

French territorial ambitions in North America were to be a major concern in the formation of the Dominion and Territory of New England. The first step towards the creation of the dominion was the move against the charter of Massachusetts in 1684. Although the revocation of the charter was undertaken in the last year of Charles II's reign, it seems to have been initiated by James. As proprietor of New York he had a personal concern in the affairs of the Bay colony since his brother had attached Martha's Vineyard and Nantucket to his proprietorship. Edgarstown on Martha's Vineyard was named after Edgar, a son he had by his first wife, who died in 1671 at the age of 4. Representatives from both islands actually went to the assembly in New York when it met in 1683.

James took a particular interest in the reports which Edward Randolph brought to England that same year, which accused Massachusetts of flagrant breaches of the Navigation Acts, whereby the Crown had been virtually robbed of customs revenues by systematic smuggling. Randolph had been given a roving commission to investigate abuses of the system which required colonial exports, especially the staple crops of sugar and tobacco, to be exported directly to England where they paid customs duties. New England merchants came under his scrutiny as they were alleged to be especially guilty of flouting the regulations.

It was on the basis of his indictment that the Bay colony was obliged to forfeit its charter. It had been issued by Charles I in 1629 to the Massachusetts Bay company. The Puritans who presided over the settlement of the Bay had adapted a charter intended for a trading company into a constitution for a colony. Thus their assembly was called the

General Court, as if it were the governing body of a commercial concern. This made the colonists vulnerable to an investigation into how they justified their authority, especially since they were held to have used it to establish a quasi-independent republic. Thus the freemen elected the governor and council of Massachusetts. After the charter was recalled, governors were nominated by the king. Massachusetts became a royal colony, and, just to show that he meant to bring it to heel, the king appointed Colonel Percy Kirk, former governor of the outpost of Tangier, as its new governor. To the governorship of Massachusetts were added those of Plymouth, until then a separate colony, and New Hampshire. Kirk was to govern without an assembly, only convening a council of his own choice.

While he had been prepared to concede an assembly to New York, James considered the General Court in Boston to be inimical to his interests. This was partly ideological. James regarded the Puritans of New England to be republicans who had opposed his father in the civil wars. He would be confirmed in his suspicion of their loyalty by the news that they had greeted a rumour that Monmouth's rebellion had succeeded with wild rejoicing. 'Not one minister opened his lips to pray for the King, hoping that the time of their deliverance from monarchy and popery was at hand.'[9] When they learned the truth, and that Kirk, their intended governor, had been the most brutal in the suppression of the rebellion, their worst fears of his appointment were confirmed. They expressed their concern that a military governor, rumoured to be raising a regiment to accompany him, was destined to rule over them. In the event, however, James retained the Colonel's services in England and a New Englander, Joseph Dudley, was appointed instead. Dudley nevertheless presided over Massachusetts as a royal governor, nominated by the king. His predecessors had been elected by the 'freemen', who had to be full members of the Congregational Churches. These were known as visible saints, as they had to demonstrate that they had experienced the gift of grace in order to acquire Church membership. Now the rule of the saints was over, and the Bay colony had become a Crown colony. Randolph, however, thought that this had not gone far enough. 'My 11 years experience of these people confirms to me', he wrote in the summer of 1686, 'that there must be something more than wax and parchment to induce them to their perfect duty and obedience.'[10] The answer was to be found in the creation of the Dominion and Territory of New England.

James extended the assault on the autonomy of the New England colonies to Connecticut and Rhode Island. These too were deprived of their charters and incorporated into the Dominion of New England. Sir Edmund Andros, former governor of New York, was nominated to govern the Dominion. He ruled absolutely, raising taxes by decree. Some, claiming the liberties of Englishmen, resisted on the grounds that the suppressed assemblies alone could vote taxation. The protestors were arrested and imprisoned. Town meetings were suspended and the selectmen, the representatives who attended them, were replaced by nominees of the governor, most of them from outside the Bay colony. Since many were cronies of Andros, complaints were raised that New England was being 'squeez'd by a Crew of abject Persons fetched from New York'.[11] The officials who had been appointed under the Massachusetts charter were all held to have been dismissed when it was revoked, and had to be replaced. Edward Randolph, who had been appointed as secretary to the Dominion, issued new commissions for a host of appointments, executive, judicial and military. Many of those appointed were Anglicans rather than Puritans.

Andros was instructed to establish religious toleration and he zealously carried out this instruction. Congregational churches were appropriated for Anglican services. Puritan ministers were no longer maintained by local rates. Religious life in the Bay colony was thereby completely transformed. The Congregational Church, previously the only one officially recognised there, was effectively disestablished. Members of the Boston south church had the humiliation of being kept waiting in the street while Anglican services were held in it.

Andros presided over what was termed the Dominion and Territory of New England. What the term 'territory' involved became clear in his levying of annual quit-rents on landowners. He insisted that all titles should be produced for confirmation. It seemed as if lands were to be held of the Crown. 'We received only the right and power of Government from the King's charter', complained the minister of Salem, 'but the right of the Land and Soil we had received from God ... and with the consent of the Native Inhabitants.'[12]

James undertook this experiment in colonial government for a variety of reasons. One was undoubtedly to further the cause of religious toleration. Freedom of worship had been inaugurated in New York from the outset. It was essential there to acknowledge the rights of the Dutch Reformed Church after its members became English subjects. But it also accorded with James's own sentiments, and is early confirmation of his commitment to religious toleration, showing that it was genuine and not a stalking horse for Catholicism. The New England Puritans had been notorious for religious bigotry, persecuting sects other than the dominant Congregationalists. Thus an Act had been passed by the Massachusetts General Court prohibiting Quakers from proselytising, the punishment for a third offence being death. Charles II had protested against the intolerance of the Bay colony. James insisted upon complete toleration and broke the Puritan monopoly of worship. Connecticut, though more tolerant than Massachusetts, resented this move too as it disestablished its Congregational Churches. Only Rhode Island, which practised religious toleration, welcomed it. Another motive was to enforce the navigation laws which New England flagrantly violated. Andros was required to do this, and did so by reducing to just five the number of ports where customs could be cleared, and having all breaches of the laws tried in admiralty courts without juries.

But the most pressing motive was defence. The frontier with New France was very vulnerable. This became a particularly urgent problem in 1687 when the French attacked the Indians in the Mohawk river valley who were allies of the English, who used them as a buffer against raids from Canada. James reacted to this threat by incorporating New York and New Jersey in the Dominion and Territory of New England. As William Blathwayt, the auditor of Crown revenues, observed in March 1688, the extension of the Dominion from Maine to the Delaware Bay 'will be terrible to the French'.[13] Andros remained the governor of the whole, but Dongan was replaced in New York by Francis Nicholson, who served as Andros's deputy. In New Jersey the Dominion assumed the right of government which the proprietors had become accustomed to enjoy since 1680, albeit on shaky grounds. As in New York, the assemblies were suspended. 'In the eyes of New Englanders', concludes Richard Johnson, 'the Dominion steadily assumed all the trappings of a despotism. Besides a "standing army" of English soldiers, censorship was imposed on the press, [and] men committed to prison without benefit of bail or jury trial.'[14]

Arbitrary power was associated with popery in New England and New York, just as it was across the Atlantic. Andros and his deputy Nicholson were suspected of being crypto-Catholics. Nicholson had taken over from Dongan, who was a Catholic, and had retained his chaplain as well as two Catholic officers in the militia. It was later claimed on oath that he had been seen in England accompanying James to Mass, and had been 'on his knees before the altar in a Papist Chapel'.[15] It was even alleged that the agents of the Dominion were in league with the Catholic French to impose Catholicism on James's American subjects, just as the king himself was accused of seeking to impose it on his English subjects. But the most strik- ing 'proof' that there was a popish plot to enslave the American colonies came not from within the Dominion but from Maryland, a proprietary colony where the Catholic Lord Baltimore was proprietor.

Baltimore was in England during James's reign, and in 1688 appointed a deputy in Maryland, a fellow Catholic, William Joseph. Although Joseph did not suppress the assembly, he treated it to a tirade on the divine right of kings. The Protestant majority resented this lecture, and suspected the intentions of the deputy when he called in public arms, allegedly for repair. Led by John Coode they formed 'an association in arms for the defence of the Protestant Religion'. This Protestant Association threw off the Catholic proprietor's yoke and declared for William and Mary when they learned of the outcome of the Glorious Revolution in England.

News of the ousting of James II and his replacement by his daughter and son-in-law was slow to arrive in America. It took nearly three months for certain intelligence of the crucial events, as distinct from rumours, to reach the seaboard colonies. Not until they were certain that the Revolution had been successful did the opponents of the Dominion rise up against Andros in Boston and Nicholson in New York.

The scale of the uprising in Massachusetts was so great as to demon- strate that James had alienated the majority of his subjects in New as well as in Old England. His role in the seizure of the Bay colony's charter in 1684 had already forfeited any support from the Puritans before the Dominion provoked opposition from most of the other colonists. The saints sought the restoration of their former rule. They took heart when James himself dropped his earlier rejection of English nonconformists on the grounds that they were crypto-republicans and openly allied with them against Anglicans. Hoping that this would make him more sym- pathetic to their plight, they encouraged Increase Mather to go to England in the spring of 1688 to lobby for the restitution of the charter. On arrival there, Mather was encouraged by William Penn, no friend of Andros or of Randolph, to entertain expectations of a favourable reception from the king. When Mather had an audience with James in June he took the opportunity to complain about Andros's intolerant dealings with the Puritans of Massachusetts. James asked him to put their grievances into a petition. Mather took it upon himself to petition not only for the full benefits of the Declaration of Indulgence to be extended to New England, along with guarantees for property rights against arbitrary seizures, but also for a representative assembly to be restored to give the colonists' consent to taxation. Before the petition was presented to the king, Sunderland had removed from it all references to representation. When he received the amended version in July, James promised to take it into his consideration. Later he assured Mather that he would implement his Declaration of Indulgence in New England. When he panicked on hearing the news of William's impending invasion, and began to restore borough charters, Mather was jubilant, expecting the restoration of colonial charters too. He prepared the ground by publishing a tract in late September, *New England vindicated from the unjust aspersions*. But it was not to be. Although James granted him a final audience in October he had more pressing things on his mind than Mather's obsessions. And when William replaced him on the throne he showed himself no more willing to accede to his request. The Massachusetts charter was never restored. Instead a new one was issued in 1691 making it a Crown colony, and granting the right of election to the General Court not to the visible saints but to the freemen at large.

This went a long way towards realising the aspirations of the majority of those who had opposed the Dominion. They had no more liking for the rule of the saints than for that of Andros. The suppression of town meetings and the General Court meant that they were not subject to Puritan selectmen and assemblymen. They were therefore less minded to look to James for the redress of their grievances than were the Puritans. But they seized the opportunity presented by William's replacing James to seek a better deal from the new regime.

As in Massachusetts so in New York two elements emerged in opposition to the Dominion. There was a motley group of Dutch and English artisans and tradesmen who were alienated from the Anglo-Dutch elite. These had no particular brief for a representative assembly, having been largely excluded from voting for that body when it had been elected. The Dutch had no tradition of participating in town or colonial government anyway. The second consisted mainly of the English business and professional community. These had been vociferous in demands for an assembly throughout the period of the Dominion. There were therefore class, ethnic and ideological differences between the two. The first came to be led by

Jacob Leisler, a German who had married a Dutch widow. He led a coup which took control of the New York city militia, forcing governor Nicholson to flee to England. When a letter came in December 1689 from the Williamite regime in England addressed to Nicholson 'or such as for the time being do take care for the preservation of their Majesties' peace', Leisler assumed the governorship. He failed to call an assembly, however, and raised taxes citing the authority of that which had met in 1683. His actions seemed to the second group as arbitrary as that of the Dominion. They appealed to William III to send them a governor to replace Leisler. Leisler himself hoped that a Dutch monarch would sympathise with his constituency. Instead William listened more to Nicholson than to the agent Leisler sent to plead his case. He even appointed the former governor of New York to the governorship of Virginia, and sent Colonel Henry Sloughter to replace him in his former post. On arriving in New York, Sloughter arrested Leisler, had him tried for treason, and executed. His ghost continued to haunt New York politics for a generation, the colony being divided into Leislerians and anti-Leislerians who approximated to the whigs and tories of post-Revolution England. Thus when the whig Lord Bellomont became governor in 1698 he nominated former supporters of Leisler to his council. Former opponents were brought to trial in 1702. It was not until 1710 that the divisions were healed. The impact of James II's Dominion of New England thus created fissures in New York society which experienced after-shocks for two decades.

Notes and references

1 Quoted in R. Ritchie, *The Duke's Province* (Chapel Hill, 1977), p. 34.

2 Ritchie, pp. 101–2.

3 Penn, *The Case of New Jersey stated*, quoted in Mary K. Geiter, 'The Restoration crisis and the launching of Pennsylvania 1679–81', *English Historical Review*, vol. cxii (1997), 311.

4 C. M. Andrews, *The Colonial Period of American History* (4 vols, New Haven, 1964), iii, 113.

5 Huntington Library, Ellesmere MSS 9611, *Transactions between England and France relating to Hudson's Bay*, p. 59. There is another copy in Nottingham University Library: Portland MSS PWV. 96. with slightly different pagination.

6 Ibid., pp. 59–60.

7 Ibid., p. 79. Copies of the agreement were sent 'to the Governor of New York and the rest of his Majesties Governors in the Plantations', p. 84.

8 Huntington Library, Blathwayt papers Box III, BL 34 (A, B, C, D, E), cited in Bruce Lenman, *Britain's Colonial Wars 1688–1783* (London, 2000), p. 16.

9 Bodleian Tanner MSS 30, fo. 97, Edward Randolph to Sancroft, Boston, 2 Aug. 1686.

10 Ibid.

11 M. G. Hall, *Edward Randolph and the American Colonies 1676–1703* (Chapel Hill, 1960), p. 108.

12 R. Johnson, *Adjustment to Empire: The New England colonies 1675–1715* (Leicester, 1981), p. 81.

13 D. Lovejoy, *The Glorious Revolution in America* (London, 1972), p. 209.

14 Johnson, *Adjustment to Empire*, pp. 76–7.

15 Lovejoy, *Glorious Revolution in America*, p. 284.

Chapter Eight

James and Europe

Foreign policy was one of the prerogatives of the Crown which the later Stuarts guarded jealously. James personally conducted relations with European powers, corresponding regularly with his nephew and son-in-law William of Orange, and having frequent interviews with the French ambassador, Paul Barillon. Other ambassadors had access to him, but the Dutch Republic and France dominated English diplomacy during the reigns of Charles II and James II. There were two secretariats of state to deal with these powers. One, for the northern department, had the remit for the Holy Roman Empire and the Baltic states as well as the United Provinces, as the Dutch federal state was also called. The other, for the southern department, was concerned with Spain and Portugal in addition to France. The earls of Middleton and Sunderland filled these posts respectively during James's reign. Sunderland, as the senior minister, was secretary of state for the south which, since it dealt with France, was also regarded as the more important. This was demonstrated in October 1688 when Sunderland was dismissed. Middleton moved over to the southern secretariat, being replaced at the northern by Viscount Preston.

How far these ministers influenced foreign policy, apart from dealing with despatches from diplomats accredited to foreign courts, is unclear. Certainly they advised the king both informally and at meetings of his cabinet council. Rochester urged closer ties with the Dutch, while Sunderland was more inclined towards France. But it seems that in the final analysis James took the initiatives. Apart from Sir William Trumbull, English ambassador to France from 1685 to 1686, the diplomats whom James employed at The Hague and Paris were lightweights in comparison with Barillon and Louis XIV's representative in the United Provinces, the marquis d'Avaux. This was perhaps because he hoped to deal with the French and the Dutch directly himself. Shortly after his accession he appointed Bevil Skelton to represent him in the United Provinces. Skelton was a former soldier turned diplomat, who antagonised William of Orange by tactlessly sympathising with his wife's unhappiness at his infidelities. In September 1686, James moved Skelton from The Hague to Paris, and replaced him in the Dutch Republic by the equally incompetent, though more diplomatic, Sir Ignatius White, marquis d'Albeville, a Catholic. D'Albeville's incompetence became a liability in 1688. In May he wrote letters to Secretary Middleton regaling him with trivia about the drinking habits of the Prince of Orange and the elector of Saxony.[1] Meanwhile d'Avaux was informing Louis XIV that the Secretary of the Amsterdam Admiralty was secretly taking steps to equip twelve large ships to be ready to sail at a moment's notice, which could only be aimed at England.[2] On the eve of the Dutch invasion the king of France was better informed about it than the king of England.

By 1688, James was on better terms with the French king than he was with William of Orange. But, although he has been accused of preferring France over the United Provinces, this was not the case throughout his reign. His pro-French inclinations have perhaps been exaggerated because he spent most of his first and all of his last exile in that country. They have possibly been distorted, too, because Barillon's despatches to Louis XIV are the major source for our day-to-day knowledge of the reign. Reliance on this diplomatic correspondence puts a premium on Anglo-French relations which may be misleading. The French ambassador was on intimate terms not only with the king but also with his leading ministers, such as the earls of Rochester and Sunderland. They supplied him with information which he passed on to Louis XIV. What James and his ministers wanted Louis to hear was not necessarily what they themselves believed or were committed to. They wanted to keep on good terms with the French king, to which end they flattered him and his ambassador, giving an impression of sharing similar interests, which was not always the case.

Take, for instance, James's reaction to the revocation of the Edict of Nantes in October 1685. After a period of interpreting the edict of toleration to French Calvinists strictly according to the letter, which broke its spirit, Louis XIV proclaimed that it was no longer in force. The result was that the Huguenots, as the French Calvinists were known, after suffering great hardship, now had to endure persecution unless they converted to Catholicism. They were not even allowed to leave the country, though Louis made an exception for those of foreign nationality. Even so, many found it hard to leave, especially if they had married French subjects who had to remain in France with their children. Despite the official ban, many did flee to the safety of the Dutch Republic and the relative safety of England. It was only relatively safe because of James's ambivalent attitude to the revocation. He officially approved of the French king's action, as he assured Barillon, telling him that he admired Louis XIV's zeal for the Catholic faith. He also told the French ambassador that 'he regarded all Protestants as republicans, especially those who fled from France'. It was their anti-monarchical politics as much as, if not more than, their Calvinism which he suspected. He even forbade English ships to bring Huguenot refugees into England, and had burned by the common hangman a book published in France against the revocation of the Edict. Yet he assured William of Orange that he disapproved of the French king's action. His ambassador in Paris, Sir William Trumbull, did all he could to help Huguenots escape to England. James allowed a collection to be taken for the refugees, albeit on condition that its proceeds should be given only to those who attended the Church of England. Only when he parted company with the Anglicans and sought allies among Protestant dissenters did James extend to the Huguenots the toleration he conferred on other nonconformists when he issued the Declaration of Indulgence in April.[3] In March 1688 he donated £1,500 to the collection for them. His ambivalence has been plausibly explained as stemming from a desire not to antagonise Louis XIV, coupled with a genuine dislike of persecution, which he felt to be counterproductive.[4]

James was English to the core, and as king put the interests of England first. He reacted angrily with the Dutch ambassador van Citters when he publicly accused James of being subservient to France. 'I was born an Englishman and I want all the world to know it', he retorted. 'Never, no never, shall I do anything to put myself below the Kings of France and Spain. Vassal! Vassal of France!'[5] In the case of the revocation of the Edict of Nantes it was not in England's interest to antagonise the French king. At the same time it was not in her commercial interest to persecute a prosperous and hardworking minority. As we have seen with his dealings with Louis XIV concerning North America, he was very far from being a satellite, much less an ally, of the Sun King. He was also concerned to maintain friendly relations with the Dutch, not least since his own daughter Mary, wife of William of Orange, lived in Holland. In the summer of 1685 he renewed Charles II's treaty of 1678 with the States General, much to the annoyance of Louis XIV.

It was difficult, if not downright impossible, to stay on amicable terms with both powers, for Louis XIV was seen as the arch-enemy of the Dutch. His troops had invaded the Republic in 1672, and only the desperate expedient of breaching the dykes had saved the core provinces of Holland and Zealand from occupation. The crisis had precipitated a coup in the United Provinces leading to the lynching of the Pensionary, John de Witt and the appointment of William of Orange as stadholder of Holland. These posts were among the few institutions in the anarchic constitution of the Dutch Republic which held together the seven provinces which composed it. Although they were called the United Provinces they rarely were. As Sir William Temple observed, the Dutch Republic 'cannot properly be styled a commonwealth but is rather a Confederation of Seven Sovereign Provinces united together for their common and mutual defence, without any dependence one upon the other'.[6] Holland was far and away the most powerful in terms of wealth and its contribution to the common revenues. Its delegation to the States General had considerable influence there, while its leading official, the Pensionary, also carried clout in the affairs of the Republic. But the individual provinces had the right of veto over collective decisions.

Each province had a stadholder, or lieutenant, dating from the distant days when they had been outposts of the Spanish Empire. Traditionally, most of these, including Holland's, had been held by the head of the house of Orange. In 1650, however, the death of William II, whose wife was at the time pregnant with the future William III, provided an opportunity for the opponents of the Orangists to leave the posts vacant. The years 1650 to 1672 thus formed what is known as the first stadholderless period in Dutch history.

Even though William of Orange became stadholder with the help of a French invasion, he did not feel obligated to France. Far from it; he became the most determined opponent of Louis XIV, accusing him of being bent on 'universal monarchy' and seeking to build up a coalition of powers against him. This policy was not automatically adopted by the rest of the Dutch. On the contrary, the merchants of Amsterdam, who profited from trade with France, felt no immediate inclination to jeopardise their profits by an anti-French policy. Their representatives in the States of Holland were reluctant to endorse William's hostile attitude, and it was difficult for him to persuade them to support his invasion of England in 1688.

Louis XIV as an absolute king had no similar problems. Although in his minority he had been subject to opposition and even rebellion from the Frondeurs, when he achieved his majority he was able to stamp his authority on the government. French foreign policy was to all intents and purposes the king's. Unlike James, he did not even have to seek supplies from a representative assembly to finance aggression against other states. The last meeting of the Estates General had ended in 1616. The six provincial estates had been reduced to three, and those further subordinated to the royal will. Although the supreme court, the parlement of Paris, was empowered to ratify edicts, including those for raising taxes, this had become a mere ritual. Louis had not lacked the resources for an ambitious policy of expansion in Europe in the 1670s, even if there were signs that there were limits to the willingness of the French taxpayer to pay for protracted wars.

James by contrast could not afford an aggressive foreign policy. Although the parliament that met in 1685 was generous in voting supplies, so that he was able to dispense with it when it turned against him, these would not have sufficed to sustain a continental war. Any parliament would almost certainly have refused to raise money to pay for a war against the Dutch. This was despite the fact that there had been three Anglo-Dutch wars fought between 1651 and 1674. During those years the United Provinces were regarded as the main threat to English interests. But since 1674 a sea change had set in. Now France was held to be the chief potential enemy of England. The change can be seen in the attitude of the first earl of Shaftesbury. In 1672 he made a fiery speech urging a confrontation with the Dutch. Ten years later when he fled England he sought refuge in Holland.

Shaftesbury's decision to go into exile in the Dutch Republic was ideological. France and the United Provinces symbolised two strikingly different polities in seventeenth-century Europe. France was the model of an absolute kingship devoted to the principle of the indefeasible divine hereditary right of succession. The United Provinces represented the republican alternative of popular sovereignty. The French ethos was aristocratic, based on military glory. The Dutch was bourgeois, founded on commercial expansion. France was Catholic and intolerant of the Protestants, as the revocation of the Edict of Nantes made clear. Although not officially allowed to leave the country, thousands of Huguenots did, mainly to the Dutch Republic. This was because the Dutch, though

Protestant, had the most tolerant attitude towards religious minorities in Europe. Catholics, Jews, even pagans lived undisturbed there. Whigs like Shaftesbury preferred popular, commercial and tolerant ideologies to absolute, aristocratic and Catholic regimes; hence his choice of exile in Holland rather than in France.

It is too easily deduced from these competing models that James was predisposed to prefer the French to the Dutch. It is true that he was absolutist by temperament, and devoted to the military ethos of honour and glory. He greatly admired Louis XIV and the example he set of kingship. But he was also commercially oriented and, though a Catholic, tolerant in his attitude. In his Declarations of Indulgence and in other writings he declaimed against religious intolerance on the grounds, among others, that it was an impediment to trade. He thought that the example of the Dutch had much to offer a trading country like England. Moreover he was aware that the Dutch Republic was no democracy but a self-perpetuating oligarchy. His Dutch subjects in New York were not behind the agitation for an assembly there, which came mainly from English settlers. So, ideologically James did not automatically opt for the French model. And, while there were conflicts of interest which led him to be suspicious of Dutch intentions, there was also friction with France over their colonial claims. Moreover, he could not afford to antagonise either power to the point of open war. These considerations led to a pragmatic foreign policy.

The major exception to this was his determination to reopen diplomatic relations with the papacy, which had been severed at the Reformation. In September 1685 James sent Roger Palmer, earl of Castlemaine, to Rome as his ambassador. As a knowledgeable Catholic who had visited Italy, Castlemaine seemed a suitable appointment. But the fact that he had obtained his title because he had been cuckolded by Charles II was scarcely an appropriate qualification for an ambassador to his Holiness Innocent XI. James expected much from the renewal of the embassy but got very little. Thus he wanted to get a cardinal's hat for Mary of Modena's uncle and for Father Petre. With some misgivings the Pope yielded to the first but refused the second despite Castlemaine's repeated importunities for it. In exchange, Ferdinand d'Adda was sent to England as the Pope's ambassador, though it was not until 1687 that he was officially accredited as his nuncio. On that occasion there was a splendid ceremony of installation at Windsor Castle, though it was marred somewhat by the duke of Somerset refusing to introduce the nuncio on the grounds that it was high treason to recognise the Pope's jurisdiction in England. Even though James offered to pardon him, Somerset still refused, arguing that a pardon for an offence obtained in advance was null and void. Later d'Adda was criticised by a Catholic who wrote to Rome, 'instead of a moderate, discreet and sagacious minister you sent a mere boy, a fine showy fop to make love to the ladies'.[7]

Innocent XI disappointed James by not giving his pro-Catholic policies his blessing. This was because he assumed that the English monarch was hand in glove with the king of France. Although in most cases this was a misunderstanding of James's relations with Louis XIV, in the case of the disputed election of the archbishop elector of Cologne in 1688, it was a reasonable assumption. The incumbent archbishop was pro-French, and Louis wished to ensure that his successor would be too by getting one of his nominees elected as coadjutor. The election had, however, to be ratified by the Pope, and Innocent, who had quarrelled with Louis over other issues, refused to ratify it. James, who had supported Louis in his campaign, was tarred with the same brush. The result, ironically, was that he did not have the Pope's support when William of Orange launched his invasion.

The assumption that James was a client of Louis' was disproved in a dramatic way in August 1688. The French ambassador at The Hague, d'Avaux, was instructed to inform the States General that if James was attacked then France would come to his aid. James, who had been given no prior intimation of this diplomatic initiative, was initially inclined to approve of it on the grounds that it might stall Dutch preparations to invade. When it became clear that it had been counterproductive, however, he denied that there was any agreement, much less alliance, between him and the French king on this issue. Since Louis had acted after receiving information from Skelton, the English ambassador in Paris, he was recalled to England and spent some time in the Tower. The outcome was that Louis dropped all pretence of helping James to stop the Dutch invasion in its tracks, and instead launched an attack upon Philippsburg. Since this was some two hundred miles from the Dutch border it demonstrated that there would be no French resistance to William's invasion of England.

Despite warnings from the other powers, James refused to believe until the last minute that his son-in-law was planning an invasion. In August 1688 the experienced diplomat Usson de Bonrepos made a special visit to

England to apprise the king of his danger, and urged him to take steps to meet it. Besides the French, others alerted James to the imminence of an attack, among them the papal envoy d'Adda who told him of William's intentions on 31 August. But the king chose not to believe these warnings.

His correspondence with William of Orange had perhaps lulled him into a false sense of security. While his own letters were brief, they were far from curt. On the contrary, with their frequent references to hunting and the health of members of the family, they were cordial. The occasional jarring note, such as the harbouring of disaffected subjects in the Dutch Republic, only temporarily interrupted their normal cordiality. But over time they document that the relationship was becoming increasingly strained. When Louis XIV annexed the principality of Orange in southern France, from which William derived his title, William asked James to join him in protesting to the French king. James duly obliged, even though Barillon warned him not to ask something which Louis was not prepared to give. Early in 1686 James wrote to William to say that he had done all he could and could do no more short of war, which was unthinkable on such a pretext. William was angered, and even suspected that his father-in-law was in league with Louis against him. These suspicions grew when van Citters, the Dutch ambassador to England, claimed that James, along with his Catholic advisers, planned to attack the Dutch. Although James protested that this was chimerical the incident led William to be cool towards him.

He was even cooler to an overture made to him by James that he would support the repeal of the Test Act. William Penn was despatched to The Hague in 1686 to sound out the prince's views on this contentious issue. William replied that, though he was opposed to persecution, and would tolerate Catholics as well as dissenters, he strongly felt that the Test Act was an essential bulwark of the established church and did not favour its repeal. James nevertheless persisted, getting d'Albeville to raise the issue with William in 1687. The prince insisted 'that he would never consent to the repeal of those laws which had been enacted for the support and safety of the Protestant religion and that his conscience would not let him consent, even if by doing so he might gain not only the kingdom of England but the empire of the world'.[8] James urged Dyjkvelt, an emissary sent by the States General, to persuade William that the Test Act injured the royal prerogative of appointing ministers and that its repeal would benefit the monarchy under William and Mary when they came to the throne. But it was to no avail. Under cover of his official visit, Dyjkvelt contacted many leading political figures in England and reassured them that William did not support the king's religious policies.

Even then James did not give up. He even tried to convert his daughter Mary to Catholicism. When she married William of Orange in 1677 it had been very much a diplomatic match. Charles II was being urged by his chief minister the earl of Danby to ally with the Dutch to offset his reliance upon Louis XIV. James himself had not approved. After he became king, however, he was well aware that his efforts to put Catholics on a par with Anglicans would be completely undone when his Protestant daughter succeeded, for Mary openly displayed her disapproval of his plans. Thus she intervened in favour of Bishop Compton of London when her father used the commission for ecclesiastical causes to suspend him from his spiritual duties. She also gave £200 to the ejected Fellows of Magdalen College, Oxford. When James issued the Declaration of Indulgence she endorsed her husband's objections to it. Their views were made public in *Pensionary Fagel's Letter to James Stewart* 'giving an account of the Prince and Princess of Orange's thoughts concerning the repeal of the Test and Penal Laws'. Stewart, a Scottish Presbyterian, had been a whig refugee in Holland until the Declaration of Indulgence persuaded him to return home. He then entered into correspondence, apparently at the king's instigation, with Carstares, a fellow Scot still resident in the Dutch Republic. Carstares revealed the contents of the letters, which extolled the benefits of toleration, to Gaspar Fagel, the Pensionary of Holland. Fagel in turn showed them to William. The prince decided to make his views on the issue of the test clear in a pamphlet purporting to be a reply from Fagel to Stewart. This was published in Dutch and translated by Burnet as *Pensionary Fagel's Letter to James Stewart*. Dated Amsterdam, 4 November 1687, William of Orange's birthday, it gave 'an account of the Prince and Princess of Orange's thoughts concerning the repeal of the Test and penal laws'. 'Their highnesses have often declared', Fagel assured Stewart, 'that no Christian ought to be persecuted for his conscience.' They therefore offered 'full liberty of conscience' even to Catholics. But they were not prepared to agree to the repeal of the Test Acts.[9]

In view of these gestures in support of that church it is surprising that James sought to convert his daughter to Catholicism. Nevertheless, in November 1687 he wrote to her a letter explaining why he had converted from the Anglican to the Catholic Church. She replied that 'though she had come young out of England, yet she had not left behind her either the desire of being well informed, or the means for it. She had furnished her self with books, and had those about her who might clear any doubts to her.'[10] Burnet, who acted as her spiritual adviser, read the king's letter and helped her to compose a reply. 'Thus . . . she gave him the trouble of a long account of the grounds upon which she was persuaded of the truth of her religion; in which she was so fully satisfied, that she trusted by the grace of God that she should spend the rest of her days in it.'[11] James replied with a reading list of relevant books, recommending her to discuss them with an English Jesuit, Father Morgan, who was then in The Hague. Mary undertook to read the books but not to see Morgan, on the grounds that conferences with a Jesuit would not be kept secret and that news about them would do her a great deal of harm. Mary informed her sister Anne, Bishop Compton and the archbishop of Canterbury of her father's attempts to convert her. These included his sending her the printed account of her own mother's conversion before she died. James's efforts ended early in 1688 when Mary protested against the recall of the Anglo-Dutch brigade from the Netherlands.

The brigade consisted of six British regiments in the pay of the States General, an arrangement which went back to Elizabeth's reign. When James asked for them to be sent to England at the time of Monmouth's rebellion, William had encouraged the States General to despatch them. The prince was not pleased, however, when James urged the appointment of the Catholic earl of Carlingford to the command of the brigade in 1686. William refused to accept him, and the issue was unresolved when James asked for the regiments to be sent to England. William put pressure on the States General to resist their recall. Only officers were allowed to leave if they chose to do so. Those willing to stay, and all the lower ranks, were to remain in the Republic. The correspondence survived this crisis, but it was noticeably cooler thereafter. James changed his customary concluding remark 'you shall find me as kind to you as you can desire' to the rather more ambiguous 'you shall find me as kind to you as you can expect'. The cool response in Holland to the birth of the Prince of Wales in June, when William and Mary seemed to go along with the myth that he was a sup-postitious child, did nothing to improve relations. Yet James continued to correspond until 17 September, when he wrote his last private letter to William, endorsing it as usual 'for my sone, the Prince of Orange'.[12] When he next wrote to him, on 1 December, it was a formal letter signed by himself and Secretary Middleton. The fact that it was in French upset the prince, since the king had been used to writing to him in English. That he had meanwhile invaded England at the head of an army, and challenged his father-in-law to battle, had brought the niceties of family correspondence to a grinding halt.

William's Declaration, issued from The Hague on 20 September, gave religion as the main motive for his actions.[13]

> It is both certain and evident to all men that the publick peace and happiness of any state or kingdom cannot be preserved where the law, liberties and customs, established by the lawful authority in it, are openly transgressed and annulled; more especially where the alteration of religion is endeavoured, and that a religion, which is contrary to law, is endeavoured to be introduced; upon which those who are most immediately concerned in it are indispensibly bound to endeavour to preserve and maintain the established laws, liberties and customs, and above all the religion and worship of God that is established among them, and to take such an effectual care, that the inhabitants of the said state or kingdom may neither be deprived of their religion, nor of their civil rights.

The Declaration blamed the king's advisers rather than James himself for policies which had overturned the religion, laws and liberties of his subjects. They had advised him to exercise his dispensing and suspending powers to get round the penal laws and Test Act in order to place Catholics on an equal footing with Anglicans. Dispensations had been given to individuals to make them immune from prosecution for holding office, despite the Test Act confining office holding to communicating Anglicans. The penal laws had been generally suspended by Declarations of Indulgence issued in 1687 and 1688 which were virtual edicts of toleration. The fiction that it was evil ministers, and not the king himself, who had devised the arbitrary policies was upheld with the Declaration's claim that they had revived a commission for ecclesiastical causes, which had suspended the bishop of London from the exercise of his episcopal duties, and had deprived the Fellows of Magdalen College, Oxford, of their Fellowships for not electing a Catholic as their President. 'A regular plan had been carried on for the establishment of popery in England; for monasteries and convents had been erected, colleges of Jesuits founded, popish churches and chapels openly built, public stations crowded with papists, and a person who was a papist, a priest and a Jesuit [Father Petre] avowed to be one of the King's ministers of state.' The judiciary had been purged, and finally an attempt had been made to pack parliament, 'the last and great remedy for all those evils'. 'Therefore', the Declaration concluded, 'we have thought fit to go over to England and to carry over with us a force sufficient by the blessing of God, to defend us from the violence of those evil Counsellors.'

William's invasion of England was a gamble which paid off beyond his wildest expectations. For much as he might have hoped to wrest the crown from James's head, this could not conceivably have been the main aim of the expedition. It is only with the benefit of hindsight that an outside chance can be made to be a major objective. Of course, the prince did not come just to ensure that a free parliament would meet and bring James to his senses, which was the declared motive of his expedition. It was to settle scores with Louis XIV rather than with James II that William took the incredible risk of sailing with a taskforce down the English Channel late in the year when the campaigning season was usually over.

Louis was perceived by his contemporaries in much the same way as Napoleon or even Hitler were viewed later. His territorial ambitions seemed boundless. He had alienated William of Orange by his flagrant disregard of boundaries. The French king annexed the principality of Orange in the south of France from which William derived his title. More seriously, he had threatened to overrun the Dutch Republic in 1672, and the advance of his troops had only been stopped by breaching the dykes and flooding the countryside. Although William came to power in the United Provinces as a result of this emergency, he never forgot the aggression of Louis XIV, and devoted his life to arresting and if possible reversing it. His intervention in English affairs in 1688 was largely motivated by this ambition. As the marquis of Halifax observed, William took London on the way to Paris.

By the early 1680s, however, it looked as if French expansion could not be stopped. Louis XIV's reunion policy, which pressed French claims to territory on the eastern borders of France, reached its zenith with the acquisition of Strasbourg in 1684. The French king's reputation as a maverick monarch also peaked when the reunions were assisted by the siege of Vienna by the Turks in 1683. While other European powers were devoting their attention to the Turkish threat, Louis conspicuously refused to assist their efforts, and on the contrary used the fact that their attention was focused on central Europe to pursue his territorial aims in eastern France. When the siege of Vienna was raised it was noted that it was without any help from Louis, despite his use of the traditional title held by holders of the French crown, 'the most Christian king'. While Moslems were threatening the heart of Christendom, the most Christian king was conspicuous by his absence. It helped to confirm his reputation as an unscrupulous tyrant bent on expanding the French frontier by naked aggression.

The successful raising of the siege of Vienna, followed by the advance against the Turks which made them retreat across Hungary, was a turning point in the containment of France. These actions helped to bring about the formation of the League of Augsburg in 1686, dedicated to resist further French advances. Although the Dutch were not formally part of this alliance it was welcomed by William of Orange. He was anxious to bring England into line with those powers opposed to Louis XIV. James II was seen as an ally of Louis XIV.[14] However, the notion that he marched to a French tune in his foreign policy is questionable. Louis did offer to help him resist William's invasion, an offer which James actually turned down. Nevertheless the French could have prevented the Dutch invasion of England in 1688, and indeed until September the proximity of troops under the duc d'Humières made the States General of the Dutch Republic reluctant to support William's pro-ject. In the event it was facilitated by Louis XIV's decision to attack Phillipsburg on the Rhine, nearly two hundred miles from the Dutch border. This attack was a pre-emptive strike against the League of Augsburg. It started a war which was to last until 1697, and tied up Humières' troops in such a way as to prevent them stopping William of Orange's expedition to England.

Notes and references

1 BL Add. MSS 41816, f. 10.

2 *Négociations de Monsieur le comte d'Avaux en Hollande depuis 1684 jusqu'en 1688* (6 vols, Paris, 1752–3), vi, 146–7.

3 Robin D. Gwynn, 'James II in the light of his treatment of Huguenot refugees in England 1685–1686', *English Historical Review*, vol. xcii (1977), 820–33.

4 John Miller, *James II* (London, 2000), pp. 144–5.

5 F. C. Turner, *James II* (London, 1948), p. 345.

6   Sir William Temple, *Observations upon the United Provinces of the Netherlands*, ed. G. Clark (Oxford, 1972), p. 560.

7   M. V. Hay, *The Enigma of James II* (London, 1938), p. 224, Patrick Con to William Leslie, 10 Dec. 1688.

8   Turner, *James II*, pp. 352–3.

9   'Pensionary Fagel's Letter to James Stewart', *A Collection of scarce and valuable tracts . . . of the late Lord Somers*, ed. W. Scott (10 vols, London, 1813), ix, 183–8.

10 Burnet, *History*, iii, 200.

11 Ibid., iii, 202.

12 Sir John Dalrymple, *Memoirs of Great Britain and Ireland* (2 vols, 1771–3), II, ii, 294–5.

13 Ibid., p. 125.

14 Even his own subjects perceived him as being too Francophile. See Steven Pincus, '"To protect English liberties": the English Nationalist Revolution of 1688–1689', *Protestantism and National Identity: Britain and Ireland c. 1650–c. 1850*, eds Tony Claydon and Ian McBride (Cambridge, 1998), pp. 75–104. Pincus claims that the House of Commons even urged James to go to war with Louis XIV in 1685, citing in support BL Add. MSS 63773, f. 25r. The citation, however, which is among Viscount Preston's papers is undated, but requests the king 'to recall your ambassadors from Nemigen (sic)', which refers to the negotiations at Nimeguen in 1678: i.e. the king was Charles II, not his brother.

Epilogue

One of the first things which James did on returning to St Germain from Ireland was to visit the monastery of La Trappe to go into a retreat. He was to do this on many occasions for the rest of his life. It seems as though James had determined that, since he could not be a Catholic king, he would be a martyr to Catholicism. He was utterly convinced that his faith more than made up for the loss of his throne. As he put it in his devotional papers, written in 1696, God 'had been plesed to have called me from the pit of Heresy, and to have oppend my eis to have known and embraced thy true religion, to have covered my head so often in the day of battle, delivered me so many tymes from the dangers of the sea, the noise of its waves, and the madness of the people ... [I] do give thee most humble and hearty thanks that thou wert pleased to have taken from me my three kingdoms, by wch means thou dids awake me out of the leterge of Sin'.[1] He never once contemplated even a bogus conversion to regain his throne. On the contrary, he urged upon his son the necessity of remaining true to his religion, an injunction which was to ensure that his family would never be restored to their hereditary kingdoms. James's piety so impressed some observers as to make him seem a candidate for sainthood. He himself was convinced that 'Providence had marked out no other way for his sanctification except suffering'.[2] Unfortunately, complete sanctity eluded him, for even in his last decade he could not resist having affairs. He was alleged to have acquired two mistresses while in Ireland, and continued to have illicit liaisons back in France.

James's promiscuity was notorious. Although he married Anne Hyde out of duty in September 1660, he regarded his marriage vows as no more binding than did his brother. He was reported by Samuel Pepys to have 'come out of his wife's bed and gone to another laid out for him', while the diarist himself was concerned when the duke 'did eye my wife mightily'.[3] His name was associated with a number of courtesans, including Lady Anne Carnegie, countess of Southesk, Lady Arabella Churchill, the sister of John later duke of Marlborough, and Frances Jennings, sister of Sarah, future duchess of Marlborough. The most long-lasting of these liaisons, with Catherine Sedley, was not struck up until the late 1670s, by which time his first wife was dead and James had remarried. When, on his marriage to the pious Mary of Modena, he expressed attrition if not contrition, sceptics scoffed that 'the bowls ... will still to their bias'.[4] 'I do not believe there are two men who love women more than you and I do', Charles II told the French ambassador in 1677, 'but my brother, devout as he is, loves them still more.'[5]

His infidelities have been cited as the main cause of his crisis of conscience. In the words of a psychological biographer, 'concubine and confessor are an uncomfortable combination, and as James oscillated between absolution and illicit orgasm, penance and promiscuity, his guilt grew and he tried to absolve it by increasingly drastic and dangerous acts of faith'.[6] Certainly James expressed his guilt, confessing, 'I abhor and detest my self for having so offten offended so gracious and mercifull a God, and having lived so many years in almost a perpetuall course of sin, not only in the days of my youth when I was carried away with the heat of it, and ill example, but even after when I was come to years of more discresions'.[7] Whether the sins, which he was convinced had cost him his crown, were entirely sexual, or had some other motive, cannot now be determined. Yet it raises a question which goes to the very heart of the failure of James II: why did he think that God had forsaken him?

For James felt completely abandoned in the autumn of 1688. His high command deserted him for the Prince of Orange. His own daughter Anne left him to join the rebels at Nottingham. His chief ministers abandoned him. Jeffreys was among the most prominent of them, being detected disguised as a sailor at Wapping and sent back to London to be imprisoned. Even his Catholic courtiers fled as his regime collapsed, Father Petre being in the van of the rats leaving the sinking ship. While James publicly protested at this treachery, in his heart he must have felt that somehow it was his fault that the whole world had tumbled about his ears. He had been weighed in the balance and found wanting. Was it that he felt that he had lost his nerve, and that if he had remained resolute things would have gone his way? We shall never know what sins he thought he had committed to merit such a severe judgement, but that James sought some kind of atonement for them by retreating into a monastic routine away from worldly concerns is clear.

The atmosphere at St Germain was stiflingly austere. There were three chapels where priests held services and the faithful attended their devotions at all hours. James himself heard Mass twice a day. The services were entirely Catholic, for Anglican émigrés were not allowed to worship according to the rites of the Church of England within the precincts of the chateau. Although they were granted liberty of conscience they were also under considerable pressure to convert to Catholicism by priests. Even James thrust tracts into their hands, and warned them that there was no salvation outside the one true church. The Anglican noblemen and gentry in his entourage were deprived physically as well as spiritually, for the resources which Louis generously made available to James, some £45,000 a year, were not enough to keep even the royal family in the comfort to which they were accustomed. 'Their equipage is mighty ragged', observed the English ambassador in 1698, 'and their horses are all as lean as Sancho's.'[8] Doubtless the exiled king felt that the poverty to which he had been reduced was another mortification which Providence had visited upon him for his sins.

Where James himself was apparently content to retreat from reality, others were not. His principal advisers, the earls of Melfort and Middleton, urged on by Jacobites in Britain, continued to persuade him to seek to regain his crown. They convinced him that William III was hated as a usurper, and that the bulk of his subjects retained an affection for him. James came round to accepting that he should make an effort on their behalf. He had dropped the idea of returning home by way of Ireland, especially when William defeated the men he had left behind there and concluded the Treaty of Limerick in 1691. One of its terms was that about 12,000 Irish troops were allowed to go to France and enter the service of Louis XIV. These 'wild geese' as they were called were based at Boulogne, and posed a constant threat to English security, for it was by a direct invasion of England that James now sought his restoration. Twice he was persuaded that his chances were good enough to go down to the Channel to await a repeat performance of his brother's triumphal return in 1660. In 1692 the opportunity was dashed by the victory of the English fleet over the French at La Hogue. In 1696 the hopes raised by the Assassination Plot were thwarted when the plotters were discovered and brought to justice. James's reactions to these setbacks were characteristic. Of the battle of La Hogue he wrote: 'the hand of God appeared very visibly, for without that the design could not have failed'. When an uprising of his subjects failed to materialise in 1696 he concluded that 'the good Lord did not wish to restore me'.[9]

In fact, Jacobite predictions that his subjects would rise to support his return were the wildest wishful thinking. Although many of James's former subjects came to be dissatisfied with the revolutionary regime, especially after Mary died and William III ruled as sole monarch, few showed any real desire to restore him. On the contrary, his whole reign had been denounced by the members of the Convention, which was a fair cross-section of the political elite. Most shared the views which Sir George Treby, Recorder of London, expressed when he welcomed William of Orange to the City on 19 December 1688. 'Reviewing our late danger, we remember our Church and State overrun by Popery and Arbitrary power; and brought to the point of destruction by the conduct of men (that were our truest invaders) that broke the secured fences of our laws, and which was worst the very constitution of the Legislature.'[10]

Whether James really tried to undermine the constitution is a question which still divides scholars. There are those who argue that he only used the prerogative as a means to an end and not as an end in itself. Others maintain that he sought absolute power for its own sake as well as to ease the lot of his fellow Catholics. Absolutism is not, of course, a technical term and different definitions of it are given by various historians. To some, Louis XIV was the embodiment of the idea. Theoretically there was no check on his authority other than his duty to God. The Sun King combined executive, legislative and judicial power in his own person. His ministers executed his policies. There was no legislature as such. The Estates General had last met in 1616, and were not to meet again until 1789. Of the six provincial estates which had existed in the early seventeenth century, three were never summoned, while the other three had been reduced to instruments of the royal will. Louis governed by decree. It is true that his edicts had to be registered in the parlements, or supreme courts; but they too had been reduced to rubber stamps by only being allowed to object after, rather than before, registering them.

In practice, admittedly, even Louis had to compromise. Thus his duty to God was no mere abstract concept, but required the maintenance of the Catholic Church in France and the principle of the hereditary descent of the Crown. Many officials whom he relied upon to execute his policies had secure tenure of their offices and could not be removed: hence his resort wherever possible to *Intendants* who were directly responsible to himself and whom he could remove at pleasure. There was a limit to how far he could push the nobility around. Such restrictions on the French king's power in practice have led some historians to deny that Louis was an absolute ruler. But this is to reduce the concept to absurdity. It is absurd to measure him up to some ideal of absolutism and to find him wanting. Historically, Louis XIV was *the* model of an absolute monarch.

How far the later Stuarts emulated him is also debatable.[11] They clearly lacked his enormous fiscal resources which enabled him to maintain a large standing army, perhaps the acid test of an absolute ruler. Nevertheless there are signs of emulation in the 1680s. Perhaps the most striking parallel with the French king was not the evasion of parliament by Charles II between 1681 and 1685, but James II's attempt to pack it between 1687 and 1688. Had he succeeded he would have reduced the Lords and Commons to a cypher. The regulators of corporations whom he used for the purpose of packing parliament were paid officials directly responsible to him, and were compared with *Intendants* by contemporaries.[12]

Both Charles and James used the revenues voted to them for the purpose of raising a standing army. This was a modest force under Charles, amounting to no more than 8,500 men. James, however, thanks to the generosity of the Commons' response to Monmouth's rebellion, was able to increase it to nearly 20,000 by the end of 1685. This was a sufficient force to intimidate any of his subjects who might be tempted to follow Monmouth's example. The army was used as a police force in garrison towns like Bristol, Hull and York. These centres were in effect under martial law during James's reign. In March 1688 a standing court martial was set up, which indemnified the army from common and statute law, making it an instrument of the royal will. In September a complaint was brought before the court by the mayor of Scarborough that he had been 'tossed in a blanket by the command of Captain Waseley who quarters in that town'. When the case was heard the Captain pleaded the king's pardon, so it was dismissed.[13]

The judiciary was also brought under royal control. The judges of the common law courts – Common Pleas, Exchequer and King's Bench – could be appointed either on good behaviour or at the pleasure of the Crown. In the first years of Charles II's reign both forms were used; but increasingly in the later years, and exclusively in James's reign, they were appointed at pleasure. Thus they could be dismissed at will, and during the 1680s both

kings used their right of dismissal to purge the bench in an effort to procure compliant judges. James even established a prerogative court, the
commission for ecclesiastical causes. This was regarded by many as a
revival of the Court of High Commission, which had been abolished by
Act of Parliament in 1641. It even used a seal similar to that employed by
the earlier court.[14] James delegated to the commission his authority as
supreme governor of the Church of England, which it used to deprive the
bishop of London of his spiritual powers, and to discipline the Fellows of
Magdalen College, Oxford. These deprivations were cited by William of
Orange in his Declaration as notorious instances of James's arbitrary rule.

James therefore did increase the powers of the Crown independently
of using them to promote toleration. His subjects ran the two together
when they associated popery with arbitrary power. They continued to
believe that a Catholic king would inevitably threaten their lives and liberties. Hence the ban on a Catholic successor in the Declaration of Rights,
reaffirmed by the Bill of Rights. As long as he remained 'a bigotted Papist',
as most of his former subjects in England firmly believed he was, there
was no way he would ever regain his English crown. Unlike Henri IV, who
notoriously said that 'Paris is worth a mass', James never thought for a
moment that London was worth an Anglican communion.

Scotland was a different proposition. There support for the Stuart
cause remained strong not only among Catholics but particularly with
Episcopalians, who remained loyal to the hereditary ruling house. The
rebellions of 1689, 1715 and 1745, along with the aborted uprisings of
1708, 1717 and 1719, were testimony to the strength of Jacobitism north
of the border.

The bleak prospects in England, together with the promising conditions in Scotland, perhaps lay behind the division which arose in the
ranks of James's advisers between the 'non-compounders' and the 'compounders'. Non-compounders were those, mainly Catholics, who refused
all concessions to Protestants to pave the way for James to return. The king
should not yield any of his prerogatives, they insisted, nor pardon those
who had betrayed him unless they sincerely repented. The earl of Melfort,
whom James recalled from Rome to be his principal secretary in 1691,
became the leader of these diehards. Those known as the compounders
were mostly Anglicans who wanted James to return to the position he had
adopted in September 1688. Then he had dropped his schemes to promote
dissenters and Catholics, and had restored the Church of England to what

they considered to be its lawful and rightful place in the constitution. These were led by the earl of Middleton, who became the second secretary in 1693. He saw that the only possibility of a restoration was for James to offer assurances for the Church of England, for instance that he would not seek to repeal the Test Acts. During the early 1690s James wavered between these two options, which gave the impression of insincerity. In 1692, when Melfort was in the ascendant, James issued a Declaration to his English subjects which offered few concessions. He reassured them that he would protect the Church of England and guarantee liberty of conscience. But he did not commit himself to upholding the penal laws and Test Acts. He also named many who would be excepted from a general pardon, including the fishermen of Faversham. Even Louis XIV thought it was counter-productive, while William's supporters helped to publicise it.

In 1693 James was persuaded by Middleton to issue a new Declaration promising to uphold the Test Acts and to let a free parliament decide on the extent of the dispensing power. He also undertook to restore the Act of Settlement in Ireland and to pardon all who did not oppose his restoration. James had scruples about issuing this Declaration, which were assuaged by the reassurances of divines at the Sorbonne that it was not incompatible with his faith. Even Melfort went along with it, though his motive can be deduced from a letter he wrote to accompany the Declaration when it was sent to Rome for the Pope's approval. 'After all the object of this Declaration is only to get us back to England', he wrote. 'We shall fight the battle of the Catholics with much greater advantage at Whitehall than at Saint Germains.'[15] Middleton's prediction that James would be restored within six weeks of the publication of the Declaration on 7 April 1693 were doomed to disappointment. Like that of 1692, but for different reasons, it was counter-productive. People compared the two and wondered how they could be made compatible. James's sincerity was suspect. His offer to restore the Act of Settlement was particularly resented in Ireland by men who had suffered in his service. When Melfort resigned as secretary in 1694 it appeared that the compounders had finally gained the ascendancy in his counsels. Then, in 1696, he made the most uncompromising decision of all by sanctioning the assassination of William III. This provoked a wave of loyalty to the *de facto* monarch and grievously harmed the Jacobite cause.

After 1696, and especially after the treaty of Ryswick signed the following year, in which Louis XIV recognised William III as king of

England, James himself accepted the futility of his schemes. He reconciled himself to his fate with increasing acts of devotion and piety. The extent to which he mortified his flesh alarmed his confessor, who begged him to be less severe with himself. He was also failing in health in these years, for he suffered from his first serious illness in 1695. Thereafter he became frailer and frailer, so that the poet Matthew Prior described him in 1698 as being lean and shrivelled. He suffered a stroke in March 1701 which paralysed his right side, though he slowly recovered. Throughout 1701, however, he experienced fainting fits which a visit to a spa failed to cure. The last one took place on 22 August while he was attending Mass, and clearly presaged his end. During the two weeks that he lay dying, his deathbed was visited by many anxious supporters, including Louis XIV, who promised him that he would recognise his son as king of England. James died on 5 September. His corpse was dismembered and parts interred in various churches. Thus his brain was sent to the Scots College in Paris and his heart to the nunnery at Chaillot. His body was buried in the English Benedictine church in the Faubourg St Jacques, 'provisionally' – until it could be interred in Westminster Abbey.

That James's bones remain in France, while all the other monarchs of the house of Stuart from James VI and I to his daughter Anne found their final resting place in England, is a poignant epitaph to his ultimate failure as a king. His brother predicted that he would lose his kingdom within three years, and his prediction was remarkably close to the truth. Why was Charles convinced that James was not capable of retaining the throne he himself had studied so hard to keep? Was it that he lacked the intelligence of the cynical monarch who vowed never to go on his travels again after his Restoration? Certainly it has been said of him that 'his personality was that of an efficient but not very intelligent army officer'.[16] That is, however, very much an academic judgement. Academics are inclined to place too high a premium upon intelligence, as a result of which scholarly biographies tend to lay undue stress on James's 'mental equipment'.[17] It is true that he was of no more than average intellectual ability. The earl of Ailesbury, who greatly admired him, admitted that 'he was far from having quick parts, though he had a good judgement'.[18] As his astute mistress Catherine Sedley observed, he could not have been attracted to her by her looks, for she was no beauty, 'and it cannot have been my wit because he hasn't enough of it himself to know that I have any'.[19] 'Oh sacred James', declaimed a satirical verse in 1685, 'may thy dread noddle be, as free from danger as from wit tis free.'[20] Yet intellect is not necessarily a qualification for kingship; otherwise many monarchs who have reigned in modern times would have been found unsuitable for the job. It could even be argued that intellectual ability is a disadvantage to those who wield power, at least in England where the expression 'too clever by half' has been used to damn politicians of above-average intelligence. Only the English could have called James I 'the wisest fool in Christendom'. James II's lack of 'wit', as contemporaries put it, did not mean that he was doomed to failure as a king. Although his education appears to have been rudimentary, while he preferred sport to study, he nevertheless acquired sufficient linguistic skill to speak fluent French, and literary ability to write his own *Memoirs*.

If it was not his intelligence, or lack of it, which led him to make the errors of judgement which led to his downfall, what was it in his character which contributed to it? Unlike his brother he was not particularly devious, but on the contrary had a deserved reputation for honesty and integrity. Again by contrast with Charles, he lacked a sense of humour. Where Charles is remembered as the Merry Monarch, nobody would have given that nickname to his brother. On the contrary, James was a serious, sober king. The only joke associated with him is more grim than funny. Prince George of Denmark, his son-in-law, was notorious for asking 'est-il possible?' when news of yet another deserter from the king's cause reached the court in 1688. On learning that Prince George had deserted him, James responded 'est-il possible?' This was more gallows humour than mirth. He took life seriously. There was something relentless even in his pleasures. He hunted regularly and obsessively. Later in life he developed a puritan streak about such diversions as balls and theatres, despite the fact that as duke of York he had employed a company of actors. Above all, he was much more religious than his brother. Where Charles kept his conversion to Catholicism secret until his deathbed, James proclaimed it to the world. 'He concluded the Catholic church to be the sole authoritative voice on earth', asserted Hilaire Belloc, 'and thenceforward his integrity, his immoveable resolve, are the most remarkable political features of his age ... Through all his successive trials he not only stood firm against surrender but on no single occasion contemplated the least compromise or by a word would modify the impression made. It is like a rod of steel running through thirty years.'[21] Where a Catholic convert like Belloc found this an admirable trait, James's rigid Catholicism is held by others to have been his undoing.

Yet in the crisis of his reign James displayed not rigidity so much as malleability. When news reached him that William of Orange was actually invading he panicked and made what would nowadays be called U-turns. He hastily discarded the dissenters and other allies who had no support but himself, to turn to his 'old friends' the Anglicans. These actions lost him a lot of credibility. Previously, ever since his accession, he had been known as 'James the Just'. As an Anglican minister expressed it in 1685, 'Charles the Gracious is only exchang'd for James the Just'.[22] This was in recognition of his reputation for consistently standing by his word. Archbishop Sancroft had welcomed his first speech to the Privy Council, urging upon the king 'that you would be (what you have been ever observed to be) yourself; that is, generous and just, and true to all that you once declare'.[23] 'Did ever man shew such exact ane honestie in the strictest adhering to his word?', demanded Lord Chancellor Perth to the Scottish parliament in 1685.[24] Now he became notorious for his vacillation. It could have been this failure of nerve which James later considered to have brought about his downfall. He was a military man and did not lack courage. But this was a moment of weakness, after which his regime rapidly unravelled. It seems to have haunted him for the rest of his life. In Ireland he was torn between his zeal for Catholicism and his desire for the English throne, which meant he had to compromise. The same dilemma can be seen in his dealings with the non-compounders and compounders. His heart was with the former but his head was with the latter. As long as he sought to be true to his adopted faith and to retrieve his thrones he was torn apart. Only when he renounced an earthly crown to concentrate on gaining a heavenly one did he find peace.

James had plenty of time to reflect upon what precipitated the Revolution of 1688. When he did not put the blame for it upon others but blamed himself, then besides his sins he might have attributed it to the moment of weakness when he dropped his drive to establish the Catholic Church and turned back to the Anglicans. What would have made it even more galling was that it did not work – he lost his kingdom anyway, and his Catholic subjects suffered in consequence. Ironically he would have agreed with Burnet, though for very different reasons, that 'he was never able to retrieve what for want both of judgement and heart he threw up in a day'.[25]

Notes and references

1 Davies, *Papers of Devotion,* pp. 61–2.

2 Clarke, *Life,* ii, 528.

3 Pepys's *Diary* quoted in John Spurr, *England in the 1670s* (Oxford, 2001), p. 197.

4 Spurr, *England in the 1670s,* p. 205.

5 F. C. Turner, *James II* (London, 1948), p. 61.

6 Charles Carlton, 'Three British revolutions and the personality of kingship', *Three British Revolutions, 1641, 1688, 1776* (London, 1980), p. 196.

7 Davies, *Papers of Devotion,* p. 61.

8 J. Miller, *James II* (London, 2000), p. 235. A different view of the Court at St Germain is given by Edward Corp, 'The Last Years of James II, 1690–1701', *History Today* (September 2000), pp. 19–25. Corp maintains that James lived in comfort if not opulence during his second exile. He does not, however, refute the contrary views of contemporaries.

9 Ibid., pp. 238–9.

10 Cumbria Archives Service, Kendal: Rydal MSS 3401.

11 See John Miller, *An English Absolutism? The later Stuart monarchy 1660–88* (Historical Association, New Appreciations in History, 1993).

12 *Memoirs of Ailesbury*, i, 174.

13 *The Ellis Correspondence*, ed. G. A. Ellis (London, 1829), ii, 169, 225–6.

14 J. P. Kenyon, 'The Commission for Ecclesiastical causes 1686–1688: a reconsideration', *Historical Journal*, vol. xxiv (1991), 727–36. Kenyon establishes that the commission was a court, where this had been denied previously, and that it met regularly dealing with matrimonial causes.

15 F. A. J. Mazure, *Histoire de la Révolution de 1688 en Angleterre* (3 vols, Paris, 1825), iii, appendix.

16 J. R. Western, *Monarchy and Revolution: The English state in the 1680s* (London, 1972), p. 83.

17 Turner, *James II,* p. 234. 'He had never been given credit for superior mental equipment.'

18 *Memoirs of Ailesbury*, i, 218.

19 Ibid., p. 143.

20 *Poems on Affairs of State,* ed. G. deForest Lord (7 vols, New Haven, Conn., 1962–1975), iv, 193.

21 H. Belloc, *James the Second* (London, 1928), pp. 27–8.

22 *The Loyal Speech of George Plaxton M. A. minister of Sheriff-Hales in Salop spoken at Shifnal upon the proclamation of his sacred Majesty King James the Second* (1685).

23 Bodleian Tanner MSS 32, fo. 214, quoted in G. V. Bennett, 'The Seven Bishops: a reconsideration', *Studies in Church History*, ed D. Baker (London, 1978), xv, 273.

24 HMC 44th report, *Buccleuch and Queensberry MSS*, p. 148.

25 Burnet, *History*, iii, 1.

Bibliographical essay

James composed his own *Memoirs*, which were a voluminous record of his life. Apparently they consisted of a mass of papers which he could only occasionally reduce to order, helped by others including his first wife. Had these survived intact they would have provided the fullest autobiographical information for any English king. Unfortunately the originals no longer exist, though James himself took great care to preserve them. He even jeopardised the lives of men in the wreck of the *Gloucester* in 1682 in his anxiety to rescue from the waves the box preserving his papers. When he left England in 1688 he made sure that they were shipped by the Tuscan ambassador to Livorno and sent on to him in St Germain. Exactly what happened to them after his death is unclear. It seems that the king's son, James Edward Stuart, employed a clerk in the exiled court, William Dicconson, to reduce the papers to some kind of order. By 1707 Dicconson had completed a narrative life of James based on his papers, and comprising four volumes. These, with most if not all the papers, found their way to the Scots College in Paris. Charles James Fox examined them when he was engaged on research for his *History of the early part of the reign of James II* (1808). Fox claimed that they consisted of four quarto and six folio volumes of memoirs, and four volumes of letters. In 1793, at the height of the French Revolution, there was an attempt to smuggle them to England for safe keeping. However, they never made it. Those entrusted with the task ran into difficulties, which they solved by destroying the original papers and Dicconson's volumes.

Fortunately all was not lost, for there were transcripts made by several interested parties while they were at St Germain. James himself supervised the translation into French of a volume covering his military career on the continent during his first exile, which he presented to Turenne's nephew, the Cardinal de Bouillon, in 1696. This translation appeared as an appendix to a life of Turenne in 1735. The original manuscript was discovered in 1954, translated back into English, and published as *The Memoirs of James II: His campaigns as Duke of York 1652–1660*, ed. by

A. Lytton Sells (Bloomington, Indiana, 1962). Thomas Carte, a Jacobite scholar, made copious extracts from the later volumes covering the rest of James's life, which are in the Bodleian library. James Macpherson drew upon them for his *Original Papers containing the secret history of Britain* (1775). There was a disposition not to take these seriously, partly because Macpherson's scholarly credentials had been called into question by his earlier publication of poetry allegedly by Ossian, a bard of late antiquity. Many suspected that Macpherson had fabricated the work. Another reason why his 'secret history' was challenged was that it embarrassingly implicated the whig heroes of the Glorious Revolution in sordid intrigues with the exiled court. In fact Macpherson's reputation as a forger was ill deserved, and the scholarship of his 'secret history' was scrupulous. A more acceptable work based on Dicconson was James Stanier Clarke's *The Life of James the Second* (1816). Clarke was the Prince Regent's favourite historian, who made him historiographer royal. When the Regent obtained a copy of Dicconson's manuscript, he put it at Clarke's disposal, who used it for his *Life of James*, claiming that it was 'collected out of Memoirs writ of his own hand'. In other words it was largely an edition of Dicconson's text.

There is a problem in deciding how far Clarke's biography is an autobiography of James II. This arises from the difficulties in assessing the degree to which Dicconson relied upon James's own papers. Some historians are convinced that he gave a Jacobite spin to the king's own version. Sir Winston Churchill was particularly anxious to establish this when writing the *Life* of the first duke of Marlborough. For there were many passages in Clarke's *Life of James the Second* which implicated his illustrious ancestor in Jacobite intrigue and downright treason. Thus a purple passage retailing Marlborough's agonies of remorse for his role in the Revolution was 'one-sided assertion'. However, Clarke indicated those passages which came from the original volumes covering the years after 1678. Thus he has marginal notes to 'King James' loos notes', 'loose papers' and 'Memoirs Tomes 7–9' . Even where there are no marginal references there are long passages in parentheses which appear to be quoting from an original version. Used cautiously, therefore, Clarke's *Life* can be cited as a quasi-autobiographical source for James's career subsequent to 1678. It has been used as such in this study.

Materials by James himself, apart from the elusive *Memoirs*, include the *Advice to his Son*, published in Clarke's *Life*, and the *Papers of Devotion of James II,* ed. by Godfrey Davies (Oxford, 1925). The king's correspondence with William of Orange is now in the Public Record Office. Substantial extracts from it were published by Sir John Dalrymple in his eccentric compilation *Memoirs of Great Britain and Ireland* (2 vols, 1771–3), by G. Van Prinsterer in *Archives de la Maison d'Orange-Nassau* (5 vols, The Hague, 1858–61) and in the *Calendar of State Papers Domestic, 1685–1689* (3 vols, 1960–72). The late John Kenyon caustically summed up James's letters as 'brief, clumsy, replete with schoolboy platitudes, untouched by any emotion save anger, and innocent of any intellectual concept' (J. P. Kenyon, *The Stuarts* (London, 1970), p. 144). This is fair comment on letters dashed off after a hunt or retailing family tittle-tattle. But James could write serious letters, as that to his daughter Mary seeking to convert her to Catholicism demonstrates. Nevertheless, an account of his life based entirely on his own writings, voluminous though they were, would be very uneven in its depiction of a profile in power. For that we must turn to other sources.

It is curious that for day-to-day accounts of James's activities during his reign we are mainly reliant, not upon accounts by his subjects, but upon the observations of the French ambassador Paul Barillon. These were transcribed by Armand Baschet, whose transcripts are in the Public Record Office (PRO 31/3/155–178). Similarly, for details of James's campaign in Ireland in 1689–90 we are dependent upon the despatches of the French ambassador extraordinary, the comte d'Avaux. D'Avaux's despatches were published as *Négociations de M. le comte d'Avaux en Irlande 1689–90*, ed. J. Hogan (Dublin, 1934). Those from Hoffman, ambassador of the Holy Roman Emperor, were published with translations from the German into French in marquise Campana de Cavelli, *Les Derniers Stuarts à Saint-Germain-en-Laye* (2 vols, 1891). Otherwise there are few contemporary sources from which a complete narrative can be constructed. The principal historian of the period, Bishop Burnet, covers the reign in the third volume of the six-volume edition of his *History of my own Time* (Oxford, 1833). But Burnet spent much of the 1680s in the Dutch Republic and was therefore not directly involved in the events he narrates. The Presbyterian Roger Morrice, whose 'entering books' are housed in Dr Williams' Library, used them to compile a record of nearly a million words, largely covering the 1680s. They provide a mass of information chronologically arranged, principally concerned with ecclesiastical affairs, but also with a wealth of legal and political observations. They are not a diary but a chronicle, some of it written as newsletters from an outside source, and interpolated with observations from a dissenting point of view by Morrice. The books are currently being edited in four volumes by Mark Goldie, Tim Harris, Mark Knights, John Spurr and Stephen Taylor. When they are published in 2004 they will become the principal printed source. Meanwhile there are several sources in print which provide some continuous commentary by James's subjects on the king's policies. A tory's reactions to them can be gleaned from *Memoirs of Sir John Reresby*, ed. by Andrew Browning (2nd edition edited by Mary K. Geiter and W. A. Speck (London, 1991)). The earl of Clarendon's letters and diary also document tory views, though the correspondence is more illustrative of Irish than of English history. (*The Correspondence of Henry Hyde, earl of Clarendon ... with the Diary*, ed. W. S. Singer, 2 vols, Oxford, 1828.) The narrative of Scottish history during the reign of James VII is even more difficult to reconstruct. One of the few published sources from which one might be extrapolated is *Historical Notices of Scottish Affairs selected from the manuscripts of Sir John Lauder of Fountainhall* (2 vols, Edinburgh, 1848).

The other primary sources used in this study are substantially those which I listed in the bibliography of my *Reluctant Revolutionaries: Englishmen and the Revolution of 1688* (Oxford, 1988). As its title indicates, however, that book was primarily concerned with James II's reign in England. For 'Profiles in Power' I have extended the enquiry to include Scotland, Ireland, the American colonies and Europe. These draw on some primary sources, as the materials cited in the notes of the relevant chapters indicate. They are, however, more dependent upon secondary authorities.

The secondary literature is quite considerable if, as must be the case, studies of the Revolution of 1688 are included as well as biographies of James II. For James's life was so involved in the revolutionary process that almost any study of them casts light on his career.

Macaulay provided the classic whig model of the Revolution of 1688 in his magisterial *History of England from the Accession of James II* (4 vols, Oxford, 1848, 1852). He claimed that James sought to impose Catholicism on his subjects, and that to do so he was prepared to resort to absolute power. Since the traditional constitution was one of limited monarchy this was to assert the prerogative in new and illegal ways. He thereby alienated the overwhelming majority of Protestants, from the top to the bottom of society. They engineered a revolution not to change but to restore the ancient constitution. As Macaulay observed of the revolution settlement, 'not a single flower of the Crown was touched; not a single new right was given to the people'. Macaulay's great-nephew G. M. Trevelyan summarised the thesis in his short survey *The English Revolution* (London, 1938). James II 'forced England to choose once for all' between 'royal absolutism' and 'parliamentary government'.

It is curious how long this interpretation survived as the paradigm explanation of the events of James's reign. As recently as the tercentenary of the Revolution many historians assumed that Macaulay's was the standard version of '1688 and all that'. There was no comparable Marxist model to offer in opposition to it. This was largely because Marxist historians, led by Christopher Hill, had determined that *the* English Revolution had taken place between 1640 and 1660, so that the events of 1688–9 were merely a coda to the earlier upheaval. The result was that Hill did not have the impact on the historiography of later Stuart England that he did on that of the earlier Stuarts. Instead the leading authorities tended to adapt the whig interpretation. Outstanding among them was David Ogg, whose *England in the Reign of James II and William III* (Oxford, 1955; 2nd edition, Oxford, 1957) was the definitive survey for its time. Mention must also be made of three eminent biographies of leading politicians in the late seventeenth century: Andrew Browning, *Thomas Osborne earl of Danby and duke of Leeds 1632–1712* (3 vols, London, 1944–51); K. H. D. Haley, *The First earl of Shaftesbury* (London, 1968); and J. P. Kenyon, *Robert Spencer earl of Sunderland 1641–1702* (London, 1958). These scholars created the conceptual framework for the reign of James II for a generation. With considerably more archival evidence than was available to Macaulay or exploited by Trevelyan, they substantiated the thesis that the fundamental issue posed by James was not so much religious as constitutional.

Revisionist interpretations of the period began to make their appearance in the 1970s with such seminal works as J. R. Jones, *The Revolution of 1688 in England* (London, 1972) and J. R. Western, *Monarchy and Revolution: The English state in the 1680s* (London, 1972). Jones posited an anti-Marxist thesis for the reign. Macaulay had distinguished between what he regarded as reactionary forces in English society, predominantly the gentry and the Anglican clergy, and the progressive elements, principally the business and professional classes. Jones took this a stage further by arguing that James parted company with the traditional rulers of

England, country gentlemen and clergymen, and forged a new alliance between the Crown and the urban bourgeoisie. He thus paradoxically instigated a revolution which was ended in 1688 with the restoration of the traditional ruling class. Western maintained that the 1680s witnessed a gradual trend towards absolutism. So far from this being inevitably reversed it came close to success. Had the Dutch invasion not occurred, James might well have got away with it. Moreover, according to the leading military historian of the period, John Childs, even this could have been successfully resisted. James had built up a standing army numbering about 40,000, of which 25,000 were immediately available to resist William of Orange's troops, whose numbers were estimated at 14,000 (J. Childs, *The Army, James II and the Glorious Revolution* (Manchester, 1980)).

One of the most striking conclusions to emerge from the welter of writings which appeared to mark the tercentenary of the Revolution of 1688 was that William landed with far more men than this. Jonathan Israel argued that his forces numbered 21,000, enough to take on the army of James II ('The Dutch role in the Glorious Revolution', *The Anglo-Dutch Moment: Essays on the Glorious Revolution and its world impact*, ed. J. Israel (Cambridge, 1991)). In addition to *The Anglo-Dutch Moment* there were at least six collections of commemorative essays: *By Force or by Default? The Revolution of 1688-9*, ed. by Eveline Cruickshanks (Edinburgh, 1989); *From Toleration to Persecution: The Glorious Revolution and religion in England*, eds Ole Peter Grell, Jonathan Israel and Nicholas Tyacke (London, 1991); *Liberty Secured? Britain before and after 1688*, ed. by J. R. Jones (Stanford, 1991); *The Revolution of 1688-9: Changing Perspectives*, edited by Lois Schwoerer (Cambridge, 1992); *The Revolutions of 1688*, ed. Robert Beddard (Oxford, 1990); and *The World of William III and Mary II*, ed. R. Maccubbin (Williamsburgh, 1989). Subsequent contributions include J. Miller, *An English Absolutism? The later Stuart monarchy 1660-1688* (Historical Association, New Appreciations in History, London, 1993); Michael Mullett, *James II and English Politics 1678-1688* (Lancaster pamphlets, Lancaster, 1994); *The Reigns of Charles II and James VII and II*, ed. by Lionel Glassey (London, 1997); and Eveline Cruickshanks, *The Glorious Revolution* (London, 2000).

Not surprisingly no consensus emerges from this prolific output, opinions varying from the notion that the year 1688 was a mere blip on the screen, making no substantial difference to an *ancien régime* which lasted into the nineteenth century, to the view that it was *the* British Revolution, marking a sudden and decisive shift from incipient absolutism to limited or parliamentary monarchy. Where the constitutional implications of James's policies tended to inform the whig interpretation and subsequent modifications of it, however, the trend in the 1980s, reflected in the contributions to the tercentenary, was to emphasise the fundamental importance of the religious issues. Much stress was placed, with differing emphases, on the significance of the king's bid for toleration. Some historians argued that there was more genuine toleration under James than there was after the passing of the Toleration Act of 1689. Others maintained that toleration was precarious under James, but that its spirit extended much further than the letters of the law under William III.

Most of the tercentenary contributions were devoted to discussions of English history, with relatively little attention being paid to America, Ireland and Scotland. American, Irish and Scottish affairs were not neglected, however. The best of several accounts of colonial affairs under James was Richard R. Johnson's 'The Revolution of 1688–9 in the American colonies', *The Anglo-Dutch Moment*, pp. 215–40. For a more recent treatment see Richard S. Dunn, 'The Glorious Revolution and America', *The Oxford History of the British Empire. Volume One: The Origins of Empire, British overseas enterprise to the close of the seventeenth century* (Oxford, 1998), pp. 351–74. Dunn adds to earlier accounts a discussion of events in the West Indies. Outstanding among tercentenary treatments of Ireland was David Hayton's 'The Williamite revolution in Ireland 1688–1691', *The Anglo-Dutch Moment*, pp. 185–213. This complemented and updated the best earlier study, J. G. Simms, *Jacobite Ireland 1685–91* (Dublin, 1969). The most impressive of several investigations of the Revolution of 1688 in Scotland were two essays by the late Ian Cowan: his 'Church and state reformed? The Revolution of 1688–9 in Scotland', *The Anglo-Dutch Moment*, pp. 163–83; and 'The Reluctant Revolutionaries: Scotland in 1688', *By Force or by Default*, pp. 65–81. The whole subject has recently been reopened by Tim Harris, 'Reluctant Revolutionaries? The Scots and the Revolution of 1688–9', *Politics and the Political Imagination in Later Stuart Britain*, ed. Howard Nenner (Rochester, NY, 1997), pp. 97–120.

The changing historiography of the period between the Restoration and the Revolution, by altering the context in which James lived, has profoundly affected accounts of his career. Until recently, apart from those written by Catholics, most biographies were heavily influenced by the adverse view of the king taken by Lord Macaulay in his *History of England from the Accession of James II*, ed. Sir Charles Firth (6 volumes, 1913). Macaulay depicted James as a bigoted, cruel martinet, one bent upon forcing Catholicism upon his Protestant subjects. His resort to toleration was insincere, forced upon him by political expediency.

A similarly cynical view of the king's character and motives is the main drawback of the otherwise impressive study by F. C. Turner, *James II* (London, 1948), the most thorough of earlier treatments of the king. It was based, in the author's words, 'entirely on original authorities'. These included archival as well as published sources. He also acknowledged his debt to Macaulay, 'complacent in his Victorianism and with all the prejudices of his period, especially those of the Whig party, completely unjudicial in his treatment of individuals, but amazingly accurate in the realm of fact and succeeding, in spite of his faults, in giving a balanced and very readable account of the events which led up to the Revolution'.

More sympathetic interpretations of James's motives were advanced not surprisingly by Catholic historians. Hilaire Belloc, a Catholic convert himself, countered the whig version of the king in his *James the Second* (London, 1928). Another biography more in tune with James's Catholicism than were whig historians was M. V. Hay's *The Enigma of James the Second* (London, 1938). These works, however, remained outside the mainstream. Serious revisionism on the history of James's reign began with Maurice Ashley's *James II* (London, 1977). It was continued in what remains the best account of the reign, John Miller's *James II: A study in kingship* (London, 1978; Yale edition, 2000). Both maintain that James was sincere in his protestations of toleration, and merely wanted to create a level playing field for Catholics and dissenters in their controversies with the dominant Anglicans. Miller insists that this was his only major objective, and that in so far as he resorted to the royal prerogative to achieve it, that was a means to an end and not an end in itself. Ashley and Miller follow Turner in detecting a deterioration in James's personality and ability after he became king, though they do not support his hypothesis that this was due to the onset of advanced stages of syphilis.

Overall, James's reputation came out of the intensive scrutiny of his reign at the time of the tercentenary of the Revolution higher than it was before. His sincere devotion to religious toleration is now widely accepted, and few believe he intended the forcible conversion of his subjects to Catholicism.

Indeed, the extent to which he sought to advance his co-religionists has been called into question by Andrew Barclay in his doctoral thesis 'The impact of James II on the departments of the royal household' (Cambridge University, 1994). Not wishing to steal his thunder, I did not draw on his conclusions in the text of this book. However, his main findings are to be published in 'James II's "Catholic" Court', *1650–1850: Ideas, aesthetics and enquiries in the early modern era* (forthcoming). He points out that 'in all only 30 Catholics can be identified with certainty among James's lay servants as King ... In other words, the Protestant servants probably outnumbered their Catholic counterparts by about 18-to-one ... If conceived of as having been a deliberate policy, the introduction of Catholics into the royal household had made less headway than even the attempts to appoint Catholics to commissions in the English army or to the navy.' Apart from the conversion to Catholicism of the earl of Peterborough, who held the post of Groom of the Stole, all the key offices of the household remained in Protestant hands. Moreover there was continuity throughout the reign, with no discernible change in the pattern of appointments associated with the king's move to the dissenters after Rochester's removal in 1687. 'The contrast with James's treatment of the commissions of the peace or the borough corporations is striking ... Almost 90% of servants appointed by him were still in office when he fled to France in December 1688 and most of the others had died or retired ... These were James II's Tory collaborators.' These conclusions must revise our estimate of the extent to which James sought to advance Catholics. Barclay takes the revisionist case for the king one step further.

A recent study, however – John Callow, *The Making of King James II: The formative years of a fallen king* (2000) – takes issue with the revisionist case. Callow investigates James's career up to 1685, and maintains that the traits he displayed as king can all be detected in the duke of York. He particularly explores the claim that he was a successful military commander in his youth, but failed to apply his strategic and tactical skills to the situations he faced in 1688 and 1690. In Callow's view, although James was undoubtedly a courageous soldier, and developed an appreciation of tactics, he never displayed a mastery of strategy. On the contrary, in his actions under the French and especially the Spaniards, and in his behaviour at Lowestoft and Southwold, he showed all the signs of incompetence which he displayed on Salisbury Plain and at the Boyne. The book is a scholarly and valuable addition to our knowledge of James as duke of

York, going against the revisionist trend to argue that the whig view of James as an incompetent, intolerant bigot was not far off the mark. In so far as his image as the duke of York is more favourable than that he projected as king, this is partly due to the fact that our knowledge of his early career depends largely on his own *Memoirs*: directly in the case of those documenting his serving as an officer during his first exile; indirectly after 1660 as filtered through Dicconson and Clarke. These were self-serving, being used to portray himself as an efficient military man and far-sighted statesman, whose downfall was due to the treachery of others rather than to his own shortcomings.

However, the study is not as revisionist as it claims to be in seeing continuity, rather than a decline, between his behaviour as duke of York and that which he exhibited as king. Turner, the main advocate of the deterioration theory, himself maintained that the duke was a good subaltern but not an impressive general. And, in the final analysis, it was not just incompetence which James displayed in 1688; it was a complete loss of nerve. This had never happened before, not even in the disaster which overtook the *Gloucester* on its way to Scotland in 1682, which Callow uses as an illustration of his case. James's breakdown when confronted by William III still requires explanation, even if Turner's diagnosis of a mental condition brought on by venereal disease must be discounted. Any interpretation of the Glorious Revolution has still to take into account the king's curious psychological state in 1688.

Index